Fishing the Scottish Islands

Roderick Wilkinson

Fishing the Scottish Islands

Roderick Wilkinson

SWAN·HILL
PRESS

First published in the UK in 1994
by Swan Hill Press
an imprint of Airlife Publishing Ltd

British Library Cataloguing in Publication Data
  A catalogue record for this book
  is available from the British Library

ISBN 1 85310 214 8

Printed by Butler and Tanner, England

Swan Hill Press
an imprint of Airlife Publishing Ltd.
101 Longden Road, Shrewsbury SY3 9EB, England

Contents

Introduction

Around the Scottish Islands with a Bias

*I*t would require a genius or a computer or both to write a book about anything totally detached from the author's own interests, lifestyle, prejudices and experiences — even fiction. (Some of the best descriptive parts of a story, I feel, are redolent of the most striking experiences in the author's own life.)

This has come home to me many times particularly when browsing in a bookshop and coming across books about Scotland written by well-known mountaineers, photographers, naturalists. Many of them understandably have the stamp of the author's own background. The geologist or the expert in social history or the botanist comes through. Even the sailor or the bird-watcher or the back-packer can be detected between the lines.

I am no different. I suspect that if I ever had the temerity to write a history of England, I would probably start in 1496 when Dame Juliana Berners, an Abbess of St Albans, wrote her *Treatyse of Fyshinge with an Angle*, work through Izaak Walton's *The Compleat Angler* in 1653 until Henry Williamson wrote *A Clear Water Stream* in 1958 when, doubtless, the history of England ended. Writers are highly selective.

All this is another way of stating the obvious fact that this book is about the islands around Scotland seen, heard and researched by a writer in whom there is an angler trying to get out. Were it a book simply about the fishing opportunities on the islands, little would be served for the ordinary visitor who has no intention of fishing on them or around them. The fact that it is written by someone who loves fishing, I suppose, is a modest bonus for those tourists who *do* happen to have their rods and reels in their luggage.

The book is no simple catalogue of waters showing the what, where and how of fishing them, although the places where permission to fish can be obtained are listed in detail at the end. Nor is it a mile-by-mile travel book for the map-obsessed. Even less is it a book of angling expertise. It is simply a book about some of Scotland's 787 offshore islands from behind a fishing rod.

Some generalities first. Every island is of course different, particularly for an angler. No-one could possibly compare the trout fishing of Orkney's limestone lochs with the peaty waters of those in the Hebrides. But nature is kindly to the angler and this is probably why the western islands make good the deficiency in weight of their brown trout with the excellence of their sea trout. I doubt, for instance, if there exists in Britain a better or more formidable sea trout venue than the Grimersta chain of lochs on Lewis.

Salmon fishing is not easy to come by for a visitor in the Hebrides and even when permission *is* obtained — mainly through the local fishing hotels — the few spate rivers are entirely dependent on rain to fill the pools. And although the sport can be very good in the circumstances, few monsters are caught. Lewis with its rolling peat moors can be bleak and featureless compared with the few miles southward to the mountains and rugged outlines of Harris. This says nothing, of course, for the astounding and beautiful beaches, cliffs and seascapes throughout the Outer Hebrides where there are some monster fish awaiting the sea angler.

People live on an island either because they were born there or because they choose to do so for all sorts of reasons; the usual one is to get away from what they call the 'rat race'. And plenty have done that. The English voice is generally the voice of ownership these days in the Western Isles. It is also the voice of enterprise and derring-do among the hotel and guesthouse owners, to say nothing of the fish farmers and other business people connected with tourism.

All-in-all, however, whether English incomers or native Gaels, there is an atmosphere of quiet, sincere welcome and a willingness to make friends. Caution, of course, is a Highland inbred instinct developed through centuries of being oppressed and deceived. Again, writing with a little bias, my heart and mind is with the Gaels since my own maternal grandparents could not speak a word of English when they first came to Glasgow and I occasionally attended the Gaelic church in the city where I could not understand a word anyone was saying!

My first experiences in the Eastern Hebrides — that's what some people today still call Orkney and Shetland — was during the last war when I served in Orkney in 1939-40 and when I even found some time and opportunity between the occasional German air raids to fish from a boat in Stromness Bay. Of all that — more later.

This, then, is a book about Scotland's islands written with some outrageous bias, a lot of love and with as much care as an amateur angler can muster.

1. Fishing the Scottish Islands

*T*here is a peculiar notion among some anglers that if fishing on the mainland of Scotland is all *that* good, it must be absolutely *fabulous* on the islands. I think it's the name 'Hebrides' more than anything else which brings on these fancies of vast, untrammelled moorlands dotted with wonderful lochs and wild rivers roaring from the mountains which bring glints to anglers' eyes.

Generalities are good for dreams. And those pictures of sunsets behind the mountains of Skye or the blue sweeps of machair lochs on Tiree do more for the promotion of fishing in the Scottish islands than anything else. Not for worlds would I disillusion those holiday anglers who, rods rampant and wrists a-twitching, arrive on Mull or Skye or Harris or Lewis to fish the lochs or streams or the seas around the islands. There is no doubt about it — the fishing on *some* of these islands around Scotland is indeed fabulous. I cannot imagine, for example, better sea trout fishing than that on South Harris or better trouting than on the moor lochs of Lewis. Nor can I imagine myself ever being invited to what I call the most private and highly-prized salmon and sea trout river in Europe, the Grimersta out on the north-west coast of Lewis. For all this, every dog has his day and I have had mine on the lochs on Mull, in the seas around Gigha and with the sea trout of Jura.

Among the anglers who yearn for those mountain paradises, too few realise the great differences between one and another. Some islands only a few miles apart and each with streams and lochs can have very different angling potential. Apart from the natural conditions, one of the most important differences is simply the management of the waters. One or two of the larger islands

9

are plagued with poachers who seem to suffer no hindrance from riparian owners. Others like Harris are well-keepered and assure the visiting angler a Valhalla of waters more-or-less for his exclusive use.

Considering that there are literally scores of islands of all shapes and sizes around Scotland, each one with its own variety of flora and fauna, it is hardly surprising that the opportunities for sports fishing are so varied in accessibility, price of the fishing and the simple matter of getting there. The Shetland group, for example, has a trout loch for every day of the year. The Great Cumbrae on the Firth of Clyde, by way of contrast, has its own freshwater reservoir and the local angling club at Millport make a jolly good best of this one-and-only water in their stocking and management policies.

Lewis is almost spoiled for the abundance of its moorland lochs, as is Harris which looks from the air as if there is more fresh water than land.

There are few generalities which can be applied to the Hebridean islands of Scotland, whether Outer or Inner or those islands called Orkney and Shetland but still recognised by some as the Eastern Hebrides. Indeed, so far as sports fishing is concerned, there seem to be more surprises than predictable factors for a visiting angler.

The only two trout anglers I met on Gigha regularly emigrated, for instance, and went to the mainland of Scotland to fish the hill lochs on the Mull of Kintyre in spite of the fact that Gigha itself has a very promising-looking large loch in its centre. On that same island, I had some very unusual sea fishing at the hands of a local lobster fisherman who caught mackerel with a broomstick handle, a piece of string and a few hooks to which he had fastened coloured elastic bands. He used the mackerel as bait for his lobster pots. When I broadcast about his method of fishing on the BBC that summer I hoped fervently that no expert sea anglers were listening — or they might have thrown away their expensive gear!

While I would love to be able to say that there is a common element of Elysium for anglers on each of the islands around Scotland, the truth of the matter is that they are very different from each other. Fishers looking for halcyon days would find them without much doubt on the lochs of South Uist but contrasting widely in price and sport with the spate streams of Cloy or Sannox on the island of Arran. There is every difference in the world between the magnificent trout lochs of Orkney (where in 1889 a brown trout of 29lb was caught by handline) and Loch Fad on Bute which has been recently building-up its stock of rainbows and brownies or the little salmon rivers on Islay.

Only this year I found the Storr Lochs on Skye, a chain of trout waters a few miles from Portree and managed by the local angling association. The fishing was dour — the trout taking voraciously one day then sulking all the following day. But no-one could ever accuse that association of neglecting its obligations to visiting anglers. The boats were in excellent condition and the tickets inexpensive. What are *not* readily available are the carefully guarded salmon and sea trout waters. For these, obviously, an angler needs much money or contacts or both.

Although I cannot say I have fished all of the islands large and small dotted around Scotland, of the few on which I have cast a fly, those in the Shetland group leave my mind best with memories. The plane journey takes about two hours from Edinburgh depending on the tail or headwind and the Loganair craft seats about a dozen people in surprising comfort; the lunch is a masterpiece of service. Also free is the breathtaking panoramic view of the east Scottish coastline followed by the sixty-eight Orkney islands which form the huge ocean lagoon called Scapa Flow followed by the wave-scarred cliffs and rolling moors of the Shetlands.

A hired car is the only way to 'do' the lochs. What amazed me was the number and variety of them waiting to be fished. At almost every turn of the road there was another shimmering, wind-dappled sheet of water. My host assured me that he simply didn't know if there were trout in all of them but he had yet to find one where there weren't any. Our reckoning was that it would take years to find out accurately. Although two and three pounders are fairly common here, only the previous week a nine-pounder was taken from the Loch of Huxter in Whalsey on fly. Another trout of six and a half pounds came from Loch of Grimsta while I was there. There are no coarse fish on Shetland.

The last stage of my trip was down to the southern part of the mainland to Spiggie Lodge Hotel which overlooks the majestic sand-fringed sea bay and Loch Spiggie which, as well as being a nature preserve (a part of the shore is exclusive to birds) is reckoned by the locals as the best fishing loch on the mainland.

It was at the well-appointed clubhouse in Lerwick of the Shetland Anglers' Association that I met some of the most enthusiastic trout anglers I have ever known. Casts of huge trout adorned the walls and the monster-festooned record book told its own story of the Shetland lochs on the various islands. I heard tales of thirty finnock caught on fly by night from one standing position . . . baskets of ten or fifteen brown trout in one evening from a loch only a few miles from Lerwick . . . bonanzas of sea trout from the voes in autumn.

'Fabulous' is probably the wrong word to use about angling on *any* of the Scottish islands — even on Lewis or Orkney. But there is little doubt that as transport facilities become easier, anglers looking for fresh challenges in unspoiled wilderness areas could do a lot worse than explore these sea-fringed Valhallas.

The Pros and Cons of Scottish Island Fishing

Many anglers who fish one or more of the islands around Scotland return year after year; they consider the waters on them as theirs. They meet the same local people, catch up on the latest news and trudge over the same peat moors or heather-clad hills to their paradise.

Islands are like that. They have an enchantment of their own and they act like a magnet on fishers and their families. And this is particularly true of Scottish islands where the breathtaking scenery, the colourful history and the spellbinding atmosphere take hold of visitors every year.

There is one particular advantage about fishing on one or other of the very different islands around the Scottish coasts and that is the fact that it can be obtained to suit all pockets. Between the rather expensive fishings on the private estates of Harris or the Uists and the free trout fishing on Lewis or in Shetland there is salmon, sea trout and brown trout fishing to be had with any angler's means. Of course, there is the expense of getting to the islands; travelling by sea from one of the ferry points on the mainland is reasonably priced where flying can be pricey.

So far as accommodation is concerned, the range is quite wide — from the fishing hotels to the modest bed-and-breakfast places or the self-catering caravan arrangements.

Naturally the largest islands have the most fishing. Skye and Lewis and Harris, the mainland of Orkney and the Shetland group come into this category. Biggest is not always best, however, as some smaller islands have some surprising fishing opportunities.

Broadly, there are five main groups of Scottish islands — the Inner and Outer Hebrides, the Orkney and Shetland groups and those few islands off the east coast which have more historical and scientific interest than that for angling. Again, in a general sense, Orkney and Shetland are excellent for trout and sea trout while the Hebrides in the west offer salmon and trout fishing. The salmon are generally smaller than those on the mainland but the sea trout fishing in North and South Uist, for instance, is world famous for the fighting quality of the fish.

Island fishing — particularly in the Hebrides — is not for the pampered or the lazy. Reaching the best streams and lochs often requires some steady walking over rough ground. But all this is part of the attraction; it is truly a holiday in the wilds. And if the angler is blessed with a spouse or offspring who may be interested in bird-watching, archaeology or photography or simply being in wilderness areas, everyone is satisfied. Of all the books written and illustrated about Scottish islands, only a tiny proportion are devoted to sports fishing; the rest are packed with matters of wildlife, history, legends, tradition, religion, culture, clan life, invasions of the Norsemen and life today. This itself gives an idea of the treasure-trove of interest besides angling.

Which Scottish Island has the Best Fishing?

Of course, it depends on the kind of fishing you want. I know some anglers who wouldn't thank you for the gift of an expensive beat for a week on one of Scotland's prime salmon rivers. And I know others who don't fish for anything else but salmon. Then there are the sea anglers who haul up over the side of the boat some fish so large that you can never be sure who might eat whom. Others are content with smaller fish caught off the rocks.

Certainly there is one kind of angler who will search the Scottish islands for his sport in vain — the coarse fisherman. I have yet to come across an island whose waters have carp or barbel or roach or dace or bleak.

Generalities first. The *majority* of the islands have no salmon although those available on the bigger islands like Mull and Skye

13

and Lewis and Harris certainly make up for this. And there is no salmon in Orkney or Shetland although the brown trout fishing there is tremendous. Hardly any of the islands off the east coast have any decent game fishing at all. It is the islands in the west — the Inner and Outer Hebrides — that have the excellent trout and sea trout fishing with few exceptions.

Where you do come across good salmon fishing, such as in Harris or Mull or Skye, don't expect monsters; the fish there are usually on the smaller side although they do have great fighting qualities.

While on the subject of the King of Fish, almost all the good salmon rivers and lochs in the Hebrides are in private hands, usually held or managed by the estates. Getting permission to fish is therefore not easy because the same anglers tend to return every year to their favourite water. Some of the rental charges can be quite high but there are exceptions like the River Creed in Lewis. In the western isles, salmon fishing can be chancy for another reason — the weather. The rivers are usually spate waters which rise and fall within days, in some cases within hours. So it is possible to make a booking on a river well in advance only to find on arrival that there is a near-drought and the river is showing its 'bare bones'. This is where many of the lochs in the western areas of Lewis and Harris — and at least one in North Uist — come into their own by retaining a respectable and constant height of water. Indeed certain chains of waters are partly river and partly loch.

Much of the brown trout fishing in the larger Scottish islands is free. All of it in Orkney and most of it in Lewis require no permit. In Shetland there is a nominal charge levied by the angling association in Lerwick. In Harris some lochs — and there are scores of them — require no permit although it is best to make enquiries first, but those supporting sea trout are usually private. In the Uists it is much the same situation.

Sea fishing is another matter altogether. On some of the islands, and particularly in the main centres, you can hire a boat or even find an obliging local fisherman to take you out. Better still, in places like Stornoway or Lerwick or Kirkwall there are sea angling clubs who welcome visitors and on payment of a share of the cost will be glad to let you accompany their members on an outing in a chartered boat. This gets you out further, and usually to where the best fishing grounds are. In Shetland particularly there is always the opportunity to go after the huge skate or halibut or even shark.

One of the best and most accommodating sea angling clubs I know is at Stornoway. They have their own club premises at the harbour and they run competitions frequently, both locally and in conjunction with the Scottish Federation of Sea Anglers. Recent European sea angling festivals there have been a great success.

You can see from all this that choosing an island that has the 'best' fishing is all a matter of what *you* think is best. What sort of fish are you after? For me, fishing apart, the surroundings and the scenery are important. And I prefer sea trout fishing. And I like the lochs. What does this mean? South Harris. But you may want something else altogether.

Frankly, a sensible thing to do on any of the larger Hebridean islands is to book into a fishing hotel or make a reservation on one of the sporting estates. Yes, this will be more expensive but the facilities and the access to good waters is almost guaranteed. At a lower cost, the angling clubs and associations usually welcome visitors and issue permits. The Storr Lochs near Portree in Skye is a typical example of good club fishing with the use of a well-maintained boat.

Getting to the Islands

If you are in a desperate hurry to reach the Outer Hebrides, by all means travel by air. That way you will pay more than if you went by sea; you will also get there quicker thus saving hours — perhaps days — of your time. What you will *not* get are the seascapes or the leisurely, feet-up relaxation on the deck or the lounge of a ship as it glides past the panorama of mountains and sea lochs and lonely, deserted beaches skirting the intervening small islands that are scattered like confetti around the northern seas. It is also unlikely that you will hear the soft Gaelic tongue of the native Celts returning to their crofts or towns or fishing communities.

Caledonian MacBrayne, whose ships have been part and parcel of Hebridean island life for over a hundred years, need no explanation to the Scots. Their vessels are so much part of the island scene that it would be difficult to imagine one or other of them not being tied up or about to depart or arrive at any one of the scores of harbours around the west of Scotland.

This is not to say that air travel to the islands is a 'johnny-come-lately' affair. For example, Loganair have been flying for years so regularly that they, too, are enmeshed in island life — efficiently, punctually and safely. And, of course, they are so much quicker. And for anglers who have made advance reservation for their fishing on an exclusive water and want to start casting for salmon or sea trout as soon as possible, getting to Lewis or Harris or one of the Uists by air is the answer. This is also the ideal way to start fishing on one or other of the hotel waters.

Loganair can arrange everything for the angler who wants the best of accommodation and can hardly wait to cast with his rod and line on one of the lochs. With link arrangements from almost anywhere, they will take you to your fishing quickly on the Shetlands or the Orkneys, to the Hebrides, to Fair Isle or Islay or Tiree or Barra with all arrangements made at the best hotels on these islands.

There are other fishing waters besides those managed by the estates or the hotels, of course. Indeed on Lewis the whole island is virtually festooned with brown trout lochs, almost all of which require no permission to fish them. And to a certain extent this is true in Harris and the Uists. So 'fishing as you travel' might suit those with fishing rod fastened on the roof-edge of their car and who might like to stop and cast a fly on various waters as they go. And there is the River Creed on Lewis which flows through Stornoway and for which a daily or weekly permit can be obtained at low cost. Fishing waters like these are ideal for the visiting motorist-angler who is under no pressure to meet certain dates; sea travel is the best method of getting there.

The sail from Stornoway on Lewis takes three hours and it is then possible to travel by road down through Lewis to Tarbert in Harris, get the ferry to Lochmaddy in North Uist, motor down the 'spine' of the Uists over the causeway of Benbecula then as far as Lochboisdale in South Uist, take another ferry to Barra or go over to Uig on Skye — virtually within sight of fishing lochs all the way. Indeed Caledonian MacBrayne offer 'Island Hopscotch' tickets to suit this travel by car.

Orkney and Shetland groups of islands also have their alternative methods of getting there — by air from Glasgow or Edinburgh or by car ferry from Aberdeen or from Scrabster on the north coast of Scottish mainland.

For the stranger who wants to enjoy a week's first-class fishing, my recommendation is simple: (1) contact the fishing hotel on one of the islands (2) arrange a week with full board plus the fishing and use of a boat (3) book the air ticket.

For those who might hesitate at the cost — to say nothing of hiring a car on one of the islands — then car ferry is the answer. Longer, yes, but the sea travel, after all, is part of the holiday.

Tackle, Tactics for Fishing the Scottish Islands

One of the questionable decisions a visiting angler can make is to imagine that they successfully catch fish the same way around the same time by the same methods on the waters on *all* the offshore islands around Scotland. That is one of the problems which tourism advertising tends to create — it packages everything so that a visitor arriving, say on Skye with rod rampant might think he can be as successful with a certain team of wet flies as on the lochs elsewhere in Scotland. I have met an American angler on a Scottish island who set up a cast of flies which he last used in Connecticut!

He is not alone in his decision. One of my angling friends who fishes regularly all around the north of Scotland and on the islands occasionally swears that he uses the same cast of flies everywhere at all times and in all weathers. They consist of Greenwell's Glory, March Brown and a Butcher. And I know that he catches his fair share of trout. What he will *not* discuss is the number of trout or sea trout he *might* have caught using different flies to suit the water. Perhaps he might benefit by listening to the locals!

Too often we forget that just as geography, latitude and general conditions create wide variations in the fly life that is available for the fish on the mainland of Britain, so the islands around Scotland are subject to the same variations. What will catch trout on Islay, for instance, may never raise a fish on a loch in South Uist. As an example of the sort of surprises which an angler gets, I remember raising my eyebrows on a loch near St Magnus Hotel on the west side of Shetland when my host insisted that my tail fly should preferably be a Loch Ordy or Ke-He. I could understand the Ke-He simply because that fly had caught me many trout on Loch Watten across on the mainland in Caithness. But a Loch Ordy? Frankly, this was the first time in my life that I had ever heard of that fly being used for any other purpose than dapping for sea trout on, for instance, Loch Maree in Wester Ross.

Life for the fly-fisher is full of surprises. It was a gamekeeper on Jura who proved to me that on that island's remote hill lochs, any cast which does not have a Blue Zulu on the tail will catch no brown trout. And I have proved to myself the merits of the Loch Ordy in Shetland.

There is no doubt in my mind that a trout or sea trout angler's fly wallet should have a good supply of the regular 'standby' patterns and, for my part, I would not set off to fish any of the Inner or Outer Hebridean waters without these:

Cinnamon and Gold	Grouse and Claret
Blue Zulu	Wickham's Fancy
Invicta	Black and Peacock Spider
Greenwell's Glory	Brown ditto
Silver Butcher	Heather Moth
Kate McLaren	Blae and Black
Soldier Palmer	Teal and Green
Black Pennell	Alexandra
Cock-y-Bondie	Worm Fly
Mallard and Claret	Dunkeld
Peter Ross	Black Ke-He
Bibio	Stoat's Tail
Clan Chief	Shrimp Fly
Goat's Toe	Woodcock and Yellow
Blue Charm	Black Spider
Dunkeld	Connemara Black
Blue Dun	

It would be surprising if any local ghillie or tacklist on one of the Scottish islands would be stumped to find the flies he prefers for a loch. The visiting angler should simply let the local expert select his recommended flies in the correct size to suit the weather and the season.

In the Outer Hebrides, anything less than 6lb breaking strain nylon should be shunned. Why? The reason is that you can never know *what* size of fish might snatch the fly. In these islands, although the salmon run small, their 'take' is voracious and some will eagerly go for a well-presented size 8 sea trout fly.

On sea trout lochs, a two-fly pattern is recommended to facilitate playing a fish without the snagging or encumbrance of a third fly to hinder matters. Also on such lochs, when there is a stiff breeze a forward-tapering line gets the cast right out and size 8 or 10 flies should be used.

For the lochs and voes of Shetland, dark flies with a red tag are advised for early season fishing. Then later in the season flies such as a well-dressed Cinnamon and Gold should be successful.

For the lochs in Orkney, there is a booklet *Trout Fishing Guide to Orkney* written by Stan Headley and obtainable from the Tourist Office in Stromness which devotes a whole page to the Orkney trout flies and their tyings — an excellent book and an excellent guide for the trout fisherman on these lochs.

There is possibly no better place than an article on fishing tactics to mention a final piece of advice about fishing on the islands around Scotland. Fishing on Sunday is simply forbidden. The religious strictures in the Hebrides are very strong and an angler daring to ignore them would soon find himself being reprimanded and his life made difficult. In Orkney and Shetland, although the tradition is slowly changing, fishing on a Sunday is not encouraged. In this connection, perhaps the word 'tactic' might be replaced with the word 'tact'!

A Checklist for Fishing a Wilderness Water

You live and you learn. By the time you're half-way across the moors on one of the islands of Scotland to fish those wonderful hill lochs in Lewis or Shetland, you wish you'd drawn up a check-list of all the things you should carry and the things you should leave behind.

The first experience I had of this realisation was on the island of Skye where the half-dozen moorland lochs range from half an hour's walking distance up to almost two hours. Yet it was not the first time I had trekked across wild Scottish country to a trout loch nor will it be the last. I remember getting lost in a sudden mist in Ross-shire out from Melvaig and getting soaked to the skin a mile from Scourie and getting nearly fried in the sunshine out from Durness. And on each occasion while I was either sloshing around in peat bogs or perspiring under a ridiculous load, I kept saying to myself, 'I must remember to make a check-list. Where's my compass? Why didn't I wear sensible waders? Why do I have to carry *two* rods?'

Now I do have a check-list which I will certainly use in future whether I decide to fish in North Norway, the wilds of Australia, the Hartz Mountains or somewhere in Arizona. Certainly I will never fish any of the Scottish islands again without consulting the list beforehand.

1. Let's start at the bottom. Are my boots or waders the most suitable for the ground I am to cover? When last did I wear them? Am I quite sure they will feel comfortable after a while or so of gorse and bog?

2. Have I remembered to carry a spare pair of socks?

3. Does my waterproof cover me adequately or does it leave parts of my thighs or legs unprotected? Are all the buttons on? No holes in it?

4. Have I remembered to wear braces — suspenders the Americans call them — if I intend wading? Or if I am wearing a belt am I sure I won't be stopping every five minutes to hitch up my trousers?

5. If I intend wearing a pullover or cardigan, am I remembering that the walking itself will be warm work — and do I require it at all?

6. Although my fishing haversack is ideal for *fishing*, am I remembering that I will now be using it for *trekking* — and is it really suitable for that? Would a back-pack be more practical?

7. Am I remembering that on the return journey I may, hopefully, be laden with fish and do I have a suitable carrier for them?

8. Will *one* rod be suitable?

9. Do I have food, a flask of coffee or tea, and are the sandwiches protected in plastic or cellophane?

10. Do I have a map and a compass, a torch (in case I have to walk in the darkness), a box of matches and a knife?

11. Is my hat or cap waterproof?

12. Have I remembered to tell someone back at the hotel where I am going and when I expect to return?

Let's face it, almost anything can happen in a wilderness area. Without being unduly pessimistic, you can have intolerable indigestion after your sandwich lunch and be without tablets, you can lose your pipe or cigarettes, you can forget your spectacles and be unable to tie new flies on to your cast — anything.

Without unnecessarily lumbering yourself, my advice is to take with you every small thing you might need. After all, if the mist does come down and you have no compass or map, you could be out there for a couple of days.

Danger Time on the Lochs

Nearly every fishing season we hear about boats capsizing and drowning tragedies on the lochs of the Highlands and islands of Scotland. It is one thing fishing from a boat on a placid, smooth lake on a mild sunny day in midsummer. It is quite another thing fishing a remote loch on one of the Scottish islands in spring or autumn when sudden gusts of wild wind can whip the water to storm conditions. Spring and autumn, sometimes even early summer, are the danger seasons for boat anglers because these are the times of quick gales.

The tempting phenomenon about some lochs is that they do fish well in rough weather. 'A good wave on the water' is almost essential for trout and sea trout fishing and some experienced salmon anglers say that the fish can only be attracted to the fly on certain lochs when it is a stormy day.

For anglers who normally are city-imprisoned, the attraction of a loch in a wilderness area is very strong. It is remote, usually very beautiful, often under-fished and holds the promise of big, uneducated fish that may go for any fly or lure. The anglers can hardly wait to get into the boat and get these rods and lines working!

There are so many other attractions, too, about fishing a loch early or late in the season. A good strong wind ensures plenty of camouflage for the angler from the fish; the fish are sometimes crowding around the mouths of burns feeding the loch; it may be the angler's first or last outing of the season with all the promise of a good first or final bag of fish. All these things heighten the excitement for the first or last 'fling' of the season.

All it takes to convert this enthusiasm into tragedy is for somebody to stand up in the boat and lose his balance in the wind. I know. It happened to a friend of mine three years ago. One of his companions was drowned when the boat went over. And my friend managed to save himself only because he was a powerful swimmer.

Of course, lochs are not the only waters where an angler can risk his life. River fishing also has its hazards. Wearing chest waders can be one of them; if you lose your footing and these fill up, you are in trouble. Wading a strange river in the evening is another; you might step unwarily right into a deep hole. But all-in-all, it is usually much safer than fishing a loch from a boat — and the number of deaths by drowning in Scotland proves it.

There would seem to be one good reason why the same kind of tragedies do not occur among sea anglers, particularly those who join a party and charter a boat and an experienced skipper. And the reason is an obvious one — the dangers themselves are obvious. One predominant hazard in sea angling is alcohol. The grimmest tragedy which has happened in Scotland among sea anglers happened recently when five anglers and the skipper were all drowned only a hundred yards from the shore at Gourock on the Firth of Clyde. The reason? The skipper certainly was intoxicated (the official enquiry said so) and others on the boat were probably over-indulging.

Here are my ten safety recommendations for anglers in boats on lochs in Scotland or, for that matter, on lakes anywhere:

1. Always wear a buoyancy jacket.

2. If the water looks unsafe, don't go out at all.

3. Don't take alcohol aboard. It can dull your wits when you may need all of them in an emergency.

4. If you are using an outboard engine, carry spare fuel and *don't smoke*.

5. Keep a safe distance from the shore.

6. Seat yourself in even balance with others on the boat.

7. Tell someone as near as possible to the loch where you intend going and when you expect to return.

8. Don't stand up. If you can't reach a rising fish from where you are seated, leave the fish alone. No fish is worth your life.

9. If a strong wind springs up and the water seems to be 'unmanageable', make for the shore.

10. Don't wear waders in a boat. You'll have no chance if you go over and they fill up.

Last Refuge of the Sea Trout?

The lamentations about the diminishing sea trout populations in Britain are now so widespread in the angling press that the fish is coming into the category of 'endangered species' quite quickly. Fewer and fewer are being caught by anglers in the traditional sea trout waters in spite of the fact that in some well-managed rivers there is still a good migration. In the stretch of the Nith in Dumfriesshire managed by the Mid-Nithsdale Association, they still manage to catch between 5,000 and 6,000 in a season.

In spite of these too infrequent records on some waters, there is no doubt that the general alarm about the diminishing returns all over mainland Britain is justified.

What about the islands around Scotland?

For centuries the Inner and Outer Hebrides have been a prime area for anglers' sport. The sea trout fishing on South Uist, for example, is world famous and the machair lochs (shallow lochs near the sea which are amply nourished with calcium soils) are considered paradises by fly-fishers who return to the islands year after year.

There seems to be no evidence to suggest that the despair felt by mainland sea trout fishers has infected the Uists. The Lochboisdale Hotel, for instance, has nine boats on seven lochs — for salmon and sea trout only, brown trout fishing being organised separately on other lochs. In 1989 the best sea trout weighed 10.5lb. The three-year average is 220 sea trout averaging 2.5lb. In 1989 over 40 sea trout of 5lb or better were taken. These figures, of course, say nothing of the scores of salmon taken in the same period, or of the many brown trout taken.

There are two things about the sea trout which, strangely, seem to contradict each other. The first is that the sea trout is the same species as the brown trout except that it migrates to sea then returns to its home stream or loch. The second is that in strict terms of the law it is considered on the same basis as salmon. This distinction becomes a little blurred on Hebridean islands where brown trout, pink-fleshed almost migratory trout and pure sea trout tend to be found in the same waters.

In spite of the fact that scientific opinion now places the sea trout in the same category as the brown trout, the additional fact that they grow to weights of four or five pounds (and there is record of some eighteen-pounders being caught) it is probably understandable why the law classes the sea trout water as for salmon.

It is likely that the sea trout of South Uist provide the best fishing of their kind in Europe. This is due in a large extent to the chain of inland waters on machair land starting in the south of the island and going up the west coast for 22 miles — a mere strip or so from the Atlantic beaches. Some have brown trout, some sea trout and salmon. These waters have firm, sandy bottoms and are safe for wading. The water is clear, of alkaline nature and virtually acid-free. As the lochs are so close to the Atlantic, it is said that this is the reason they produce such energetic, sporting fish. And the surrounding machair is very beautiful, particularly in spring and summer when it is carpeted with flowers.

Many reasons are put forward to account for the vigour of these sea trout — amongst them the sudden encounter with fresh water as the fish come in from the sea which seems to invigorate them. Another reason given is that the fish find themselves swimming over sand like that on the sea-bed and they become as lively and reckless as they were in the ocean. Whatever the reasons, catching a sea trout in South Uist is a tremendous experience. Thousands of returning anglers over the last hundred years can hardly be wrong!

So far as records show at present, there seems to be no decline either in quality or quantity of sea trout in the Outer Hebrides — Lewis or Harris or the Uists. And the premier fishing waters on these machair lochs along the coast are maintaining their world-wide reputation.

The Virgin Salmon

So you're crazy about fishing for sea trout in the warm, balmy days of summer? Well, who isn't? Of course, the season is too short for the shoals of these silver beauties ascending the rivers in their mad, savage dash upstream to spawn. But the idea of standing silently like a heron in the shallow reaches of a mirror-smooth pool and casting the Black Zulu delicately into the quiet-flowing stream on a summer evening takes your breath away.

Then there's the 'take'. What an explosion! The rod is almost jerked from your hand as the living torpedo comes right out of the water and gives you the fight and the fright of your life.

For the angler who has always enjoyed sea trout fishing in these islands off Scotland which have salmon runs, there is usually plenty of grilse to delight this kind of fisher. In the North Harris fishery, for example, 95 per cent of the salmon are either grilse or fish which have spawned as grilse and returned for a second or subsequent spawning. So the chances of catching a grilse are very high indeed.

As every obsessive angler of migrating fish knows, the grilse is simply a young, virgin salmon that has been at sea for at least a year and is coming up-river to spawn for the first time. Weights range from 4lb to around 7lb.

What is so attractive about grilse to the angler is that it ranks fully with the sea trout as a fighter. If it is not yet old enough to be the King of Fish, you may be sure it is the acrobatic Prince. What always seems to me surprising is that salmon anglers who do catch a midsummer grilse tend to shrug the experience off as 'a wee salmon'.

You will catch grilse on the salmon rivers, of course, but you should know that some rivers tend to have more of them than others — at least they show themselves more. And the salmon rivers of the Outer Hebrides have more than their average share of them.

Writing or talking about specifics regarding salmon runs on rivers generally is a dangerous game since every river has its own season for runs. But as a rule the grilse is a summer fish starting its run from about mid-May to the end of August. For this reason, many a holiday angler fishing a river for trout or sea trout has had the shock of his life when a grilse takes his fly.

To my mind, this is the most natural thing in the world because by using trout tackle and a single-handed rod of ten feet this angler is doing exactly the right thing to catch this acrobatic fish. The one thing he didn't know was where the grilse would be.

For the angler who really wants to find the grilse, here are some ground rules:

1. Don't expect them to be in the 'usual' salmon lies. They will also be in the glides and shallow streams. In July and August in some rivers the grilse are lying in water only knee-deep.

2. When the river is in spate the grilse will move upstream at a tremendous rate. Fresh, sea-liced specimens have been taken 40 miles upstream within a day of a spate. This means that in a

swollen river in summer you are more likely to catch grilse well up-river than in the lower reaches.

3. The places to look for them are just below a waterfall or weir where the grilse are often packed like sardines, all of them having the enforced rest, frustrated and angry and trying to get used to their new surroundings.

Some more advice about grilse fishing is to fish with small flies, say number 8 to 12. The Stoat's Tail or the Hairy Mary are excellent grilse-attractors. Note that I say 'flies' — plural — because a two-fly cast is ideal, just as it is for sea trout. Never try three. The complications you can get into if you hook a grilse on a three-fly cast are horrendous.

As with fishing for any species of fish there are of course snags. The main one with grilse is that they are not easy to hook. Indeed, it is likely that you lose more than you catch because the fish are so vigorous and often taken the fly so flippantly that they get off easily.

You have to use your eyes and ears if you want to catch grilse. They arrive in shoals and they race, run, splash about and leap all over the place in their haste to get upstream, pausing only to 'get their breath back' before falls or broken water. If you see or hear them on a stretch of river, don't waste a minute in considering tactics or strategy. Start casting immediately as you would for trout, keep as far out of the skyline as practical, and if you get one, try to ensure that it is well hooked. Don't waste too much time with him. Get him into your net or fixed by your tailer as soon as possible.

There are some epicures who say that the grilse at table rate far higher than either the adult salmon or the sea trout. From my own experience, I do not require a food expert to tell me *that*!

2. The Inner Hebrides

*T*he islands to the west of Scotland are known as the Hebrides. The ones furthest west out in the Atlantic are the Outer Hebrides and those nearer Scotland the Inner Hebrides.

These islands are large, small, mountainous, flat, accessible, isolated, tourist-populated, deserted, rocky or sandy or peaty. You take your pick. They range from the popular, incredibly beautiful ones off the Ayrshire coast like Arran and Bute, to the inner ones of Jura and Mull and Skye to the ones on the edge of the world such as Lewis and Harris and Tiree.

Some of these islands have wonderful trout and sea trout lochs; others do not. Salmon fishing is as scarce as the rivers, usually expensive and permission to fish them difficult. But whether an island has fishable lochs or not, there is always the sea and invariably a boatman or charter skipper ready to take an angler or a group out to some of the most prolific fishing waters this side of the Atlantic. In the Hebrides there is water and fish everywhere. In South Uist there is more trout and sea trout water than land. On Mull there are the rivers and the lochs. And on the smaller islands which have no game fish, there is always the sea.

Scottish island fishing is not for the meat-hunters. Salmon — even on Skye and Mull — never reach the same weight and size as their brothers on the mainland. Although the occasional big one is caught, there are few surprises.

Another big difference is the surrounding scenery. With the possible exception of Skye, there is none of the majestic riverside atmosphere of the Spey or the Tay, no roaring waterfalls or pine-fringed salmon pools or pastoral beauty of the Tweed. The lochs on Lewis and Harris which are dotted over vast peaty moorlands have none of the photogenic qualities of Loch Lomond or Loch Tay on the mainland. Some might describe them as stark.

Apart from the excellence of the fishing, the main attraction for anglers is the seclusion. The dream of 'a loch to yourself' or the splendid isolation of a far-off sea trout stream comes true on many of these incredibly beautiful islands.

There is a real magic about Hebridean island fishing which has more to do with the ethereal nature of the places than the fishing itself. Anglers come back year after year. It is almost a spiritual experience in which the activity of hunting for fish is the medium through which the angler reaches Valhalla for a week or a fortnight. The fish become simply the excuse to visit the Celtic dreamland again and again.

More practically, there is angling to suit every taste and pocket. On the largest island, Lewis, there is free fishing on lochs that are dotted over vast peaty moorlands. And there are salmon and sea trout beats on rivers to be had at a price elsewhere. There are fishing facilities on lochs managed by the hotels on Harris and South Uist for their own guests; and there are the Storr Lochs on Skye capably managed by Portree Angling Club which welcomes visitors and supplies boats for a few pounds per day. Sea angling from rocks and beaches of the islands is very successful and costs nothing. And there are scores of boatmen who will take anglers out to sea in rod-bending trips at reasonable cost.

Although salmon and trout caught in the Hebrides have never reached the British record books, the same cannot be said for the sea fish caught in the waters around the islands. Mr D. Hopper caught an Angler Fish of 45lb in the Sound of Mull in 1978. Mr M. Lawton caught a Haddock of almost 10lb off the Summer Isles in 1980. Mr J. Morrison hooked and landed a monster Blue Shark of 85½lb off Stornoway in Lewis in 1972 and Mr I. Jenkins caught a Turbot of 25½lb off Mull in 1982. These records — like those of most sea fish — are constantly being broken.

Arran

It was a schoolmaster on holiday who gave me this idea about the Island of Arran when I was about thirteen. My chum and I were camping that year at Lochranza on an idyllic little meadow up from the foreshore just beyond the Twelve Apostles row of cottages. We decided to do a hike up the hillside so we walked and climbed and panted through Glen Catacol for a long time until we saw a tent on a little tree-fringed plateau half way up the hill. There was a grey-haired man poking at a small fire and holding a sizzling frying pan over the flames. Two boys were beside him looking on.

He looked up. 'Hello.'

'Hello,' I said.

'Where are you off to?'

'Just walking,' I said. 'To see the loch they say is up here.'

'You hungry?'

My chum nodded and stared at the frying pan.

'Siddown,' the man said, 'and have a trout with us. We caught them this morning.' He carefully eased out the fish one at a time. They were coated with oatmeal and fried in butter.

I forget his name and that of his sons, but I do remember him, and that he was a schoolmaster.

And *what* a schoolmaster! He and his boys had been fishing for these trout on Loch Tanna which was just a little beyond their camp. And as we sipped the tea and ate the fish and munched the biscuits, without any apology or finesse hc 'set up school' by that campfire and explained about this wonderful island called Arran. We were wide-eyed and gawking. I never forgot what he told us; all that was missing was a blackboard and an atlas.

'Now, if you look at a map of Scotland, you'll see that the mountains form a ridge which runs diagonally across the country from the east right down to the west.'

'Yes, we get that at school. That's the Highlands — I mean above that line. It's called the Fault or something.'

'Correct, sonny boy. Now where d'you think that Highland Line stops over here in the west?'

'Glasgow?' my chum suggested.

'No. Think again.'

'Don't know,' I said.

'Here.'

'In Arran?'

'Right. The mountains go under the sea, then there is this one big, big peak which comes up above the surface. And this is it — Arran.'

'But this is an island.'

'Right. And *that's* why all the plants and animals and the trees and the birds are Highland — just as they are further north. Yet just across the Firth of Clyde there on the Ayrshire coast the scenery is quite different. It's all Lowland scenery over there. And that's only an hour away by boat.'

Whether his theory holds water with geologists or geographers still, I have no idea. What stays in my mind is that he said that Arran was different. It is a Highland island in the Lowlands of Scotland.

To my mind, it is something else — a Little Scotland. Everything about this jewel in the Firth of Clyde is the Highlands in Miniature. There are little roads and little cottages and little streams and a bit of just about everything we treasure from the mountains up north.

For the angler who wants to combine his fishing with his family, this is where he should go. There are no roaring rivers or broad sweeps of water, no pastoral glides as he might find them in the bee-droning chalk streams of the south of England, certainly no vast lakes for shooting head lines or exotic lures. All the freshwater Valhallas will be tumbling streams that lift their voices when there is a downpour of rain and small heather-fringed mountain lochs. And except for the sound of birds, a golden silence.

Generalities first. The rivers on the island of Arran are spate rivers. Plenty of rain is needed to keep the water at a good fishable level, and depending at how you look at rainy weather, Arran usually has its fair share. The trout in the rivers are small, usually less than half a pound, but during a spate and particularly just as it is running off, good-sized sea trout can be caught. From the middle of July onwards there is the occasional salmon.

The best of these small spate rivers are at Sliddery, Cloy and Sannox and permission to fish them is quite easy to obtain from the various local village shops or the Tourist Office in Brodick.

Over on the west coast of the island there is a larger and better spate river called the Machrie, the pools of which provide good fishing for about three miles. This river is divided into three beats and the season is from June to October. Because this is a salmon river — and quite a good one — the price of letting by day or by week is higher than any of the other streams on the island.

Fly-fishing is the preferred method on the Machrie but some worm fishing is allowed for two rods. No spinning is allowed.

I was visiting friends in Arran recently with my wife. We stopped the car at the road bridge over the Machrie and I walked upstream along the bank looking at the deep, almost black pools. I did not intend fishing. Indeed, I doubt if I could get a permit, anyway, because the Estate Office which manages the river is at Killiechassie in Aberfeldy in Perthshire, and I knew that they let the fishings out usually on a weekly basis and booked as early as January.

As luck would have it, I met the gamekeeper and we talked about the river. As I expected he said that the estuary of the river was poached a great deal. He recalled autumn fogs that settled right down the length of the river and out into the sea. Then, when the fog lifted, you could see half a dozen small craft with nets pulling in salmon and sea trout as if the curtains on a stage had been lifted and the scene lit up.

'Can't anyone stop the poachers?' I asked.

'Yes,' he said. 'The fisheries control vessel, but that's stationed miles across the Firth at Helensburgh. It would take them hours to get over here, and by that time the poachers are gone.'

For all the deprivation caused by these off-shore poachers, the river is still a good one for salmon and sea trout. It rises and falls very quickly but during periods of plenty of water, there is some excellent sea trout fishing in the various dark resting places for the fish — Duke's Pool, Morton's Pool, Lady Mary Pool, Duchess Pool, Sharp's Pool and Shepherd's Pool.

While the Machrie offers no spectacular sea trout bonanzas — less than a hundred are caught on a yearly average — it is a beautiful little water.

Another pleasant river to fish is the Iorsa which is owned by Dougarie Estate and not far from the Machrie. Mainly a sea trout spate river, it does occasionally produce a salmon. There are two beats and the upper one includes Loch Iorsa where there is a boathouse and a reliable boat. This upper beat extends down as far as the Gorge Pool, then the lower beat stretches from there to the sea.

The Rosa burn is a delightful smallish stream managed by the Arran Estates at Brodick.

Arran Angling Association whose permits for fishing are issued by Arran Tourist Information Centre in Brodick have been quite active over the past few years and recently they have stocked Loch

Garbad with sizeable brown trout. There is a daily catch limit of two trout per rod per day. Not more than fifteen rods may fish the loch at any one time. All the river permit holders are entitled to fish the loch and this at least occupies an angler who is faced with a dry river.

While the freshwater opportunities on Arran may be small and dependent on rain, there is one tract of water which is constantly vast, has a high reputation for its fishing and depends neither on rainfall nor height — the ocean around the island.

Sea anglers consider the waters around Arran as among the best in Britain. Certainly in recent years the activities of commercial fishing throughout the Firth of Clyde has come in for a lot of criticism among sports fishers who complain of drift netting and trawling right up to the foreshores. However, the sea around Arran, particularly Lamlash Bay for its haddock and codling, is still recognised as one of the most prolific in the country.

Another attractive feature of Arran for sea anglers or for their families is the fact that there is a good road running right round the island giving access to almost every possible kind of rock or shingle or beach fishing. Nevertheless, it must be said that the most popular and successful method is by boat. Here Lamlash Bay comes into its own since the area between Arran and the Holy Island is quiet, secluded and safe in its four square miles for dinghy fishing. Other areas that are prolific are Brodick Bay, Whiting Bay and the Sound of Pladda and Loch Ranza.

So popular is sea angling that there is an Arran Sea Angling Centre at the beach in Brodick. Dinghies are available for hire complete with outboards. Rods, reels, tackle are also available and there are bait and freeze facilities. The island's only full-scale marine store is at Lamlash where they sell everything to do with boats and sea fishing. At Kilmory, not far from Lamlash, there are also 16-foot longliner boats for four or five anglers for hire. Whiting Bay, Machrie and Kildonan are also centres for boat hiring and advice is plentiful and free.

For non-fishing members of an angler's family, there are scores of things to do. The island has excellent golf courses (three 18-hole courses, three 9-hole and one 12-hole), interesting museums, ancient castles, good beaches, bird-watching sites, indoor and outdoor swimming pools, tennis courts, pony trekking centres. Whether fishing a river, loch or at sea, an angler need have no bad conscience about leaving others in the family to amuse themselves.

The list of notable fish caught from various waters in Britain certainly does not include salmon or trout from Arran's streams or lochs. And even the reputable sea catches have not reached the heavyweight league with the exception of two fish which are usually very small when they are caught anywhere. One of these is the Grey Gurnard which was caught off Arran in 1971 by D. Cameron-McIntosh and weighed 1lb 10oz. The other was a Cuckoo Ray caught by N.C. McLean in Lamlash Bay. It weighed 5lb. Both these fish are significant for their weight for their type.

How to get to this fisherman's holiday paradise? The most popular route is by car ferry from Ardrossan on the Ayrshire coast (not far from Glasgow) to Brodick on the island. Time is about an hour and tickets are sold by the operators Caledonian MacBrayne in advance from their office in Gourock.

People who come to Arran, whether to fish or simply to enjoy the peace of the place, return year after year. The trout are small, the few salmon are small but the scenery and the atmosphere on this 'Highlands in Miniature' is majestic and magic.

Other Attractions

One of the big problems about fishing and families at holiday time is one's conscience. Although one in eight anglers in Britain is a woman, let's face it — the other seven are husbands and fathers who have to undertake that delicate balancing act between a day's fishing on a river or a loch and playing with their children on a beach.

It is a burden all anglers bear. Some — and that includes me — compromise by fishing on holiday every *second* day. Others happily have angling spouses and even children who enjoy the sport. But for the majority of fishermen, it is a matter of consideration for what others in the family want to do and of recognising the fact that there are many people who do not fish.

There is another problem. What do the others in the family do if fishing in the nearby river, lake or sea is the only interest in the area? After all, that's what fishing hotels are for, aren't they? Fishing. Nothing else. One way out of this annual problem is for the family to choose a vacation spot that has, if not everything to suit everyone's taste, at least most things most of the time for most of the family while Dad fishes. Places like this are not all that easy to find. After all, what other interests are there for non-anglers in the immediate area of the chalkstreams in southern England? What other activities are there around a big trout reservoir like Rutland or Grafham Water? Even the wonderful salmon rivers of Scotland have their limitations in offering diversions for non-anglers.

One Scottish island for which nature and enterprising natives seem to have solved this problem is the island of Arran on the Firth of Clyde. Only an hour by car ferry from Ardrossan on the Ayrshire coast, this 'Highlands in Miniature' island of mountains and glens and beaches combines everything that an angler's family could ever wish for a holiday *without* seeing the fisherman disappear into a misty water wilderness never to reappear until the next day 'and the truth not in him'.

As an example, bird-watchers find a bonanza of different species which have no counterpart only a few miles across the firth in Ayrshire. Golden eagles can be seen regularly. Robert Gray, the nineteenth century ornithologist and author of the famous book *Birds of the West of Scotland* published in 1871 had this to say about Arran 'There is perhaps no part of the Western Hebrides more remarkable for the sublimity of its bird haunts than Arran. The towering peaks of Goat Fell and Ben Ghnuis — homes of the Eagle and Ptarmigan — can nowhere be exceeded for grandeur and magnificence.'

The tourist office in Brodick (Tel: Brodick 2140/2401) issue a very interesting little chart showing twenty birds and the months during which they can be seen on the island. Among these are the Great Northern Diver, the Greenshank and the Wood Warbler.

There is a world of pre-history, recent history, tradition and legend on Arran. The island is one of the world's classic geological locations. The local rock running round much of the island is 250 million years old. Arran is very rich in prehistoric sites, particularly those of the New Stone Age and the Early Bronze Age. On Machrie Moor there is a group of seven circles — early Bronze Age monuments.

Although Arran is dotted all around its fifty-six miles with enchanting villages — Blackwaterfoot, Sliddery, Lagg, Pirnmill, Lochranza, Whiting Bay, Lamlash — it is the island's capital

Brodick that attracts the families, the golfers, the sandcastle-builders, the tourists, the antiquers and the stollers. It is a small, compact little place, unspoilt and cosy. Behind the town is Brodick Castle in the middle of what is Scotland's first island country park. There is a ranger service to lead visitors along eleven miles of scenic woodland trails. In a recent poll, two thirds of visitors said that they came to Arran for the peace and quiet and the hill walking. The other third said they fancied all sorts of other attractions.

Possibly because the island is only an hour's sailing from the mainland of Scotland, there is an unusual and attractive combination of old Highland ways and modern amenities. While the local people in the villages run their dances and socials unchanged as they have done for a hundred years, less than a mile away from most of them are modern restaurants and hotels with outstanding reputations using sophisticated menus with local produce. This blend of ancient Highland Scotland with today's tourist needs is concentrated admirably on this small island.

All this means that Arran is an island for anglers with a conscience about their families. While he can fish any of the salmon rivers or the trout lochs, he can be assured that the rest of the family is not drumming its fingers staring out of the window of some bleak fishing hotel on a moorland wilderness.

OTHER ISLANDS IN THE AREA

Ailsa Craig lies just off the Ayrshire coast. It used to be known as 'Paddy's Milestone' because it was the outstanding sea-mark seen by thousands of Irish peasants during the potato famines when they sailed to seek work in Glasgow in the nineteenth century. The blue granite stone quarried from the rock is used for kerbstones and making stones for the game of curling.

Davaar Island is at the entrance to Campbeltown Loch off the east coast of Kintyre. In the 1880s Alexander McKinnon, a young local artist, chose one of the seven caves on the island to paint on a rock face a picture of the Crucifixion. Then he vanished for years and nobody knew who the painter was. In 1934 McKinnon — an old man in his eighties — returned to repaint much of the work and a local artist now keeps it in good order.

Holy Isle, the Gaelic name of which is *Eilean Molaise* ('the island of Saint Molaise'. St Molaise was a disciple of St Columba). It lies in the middle of Lamlash Bay on the Firth of Clyde just off the coast of Arran.

Where To Get Permission To Fish

FRESHWATER FISHING

For rivers Blackwater, Kilmory Water, Sliddery Water, Rosa Water contact Arran Angling Association, the Anchorage, Blackwaterfoot, or Johnson's Shops, Blackwaterfoot, or the Post Office, Sliddery.

For Machrie Water contact the Factor, The Estate Office, Killiechassie, Aberfeldy, Perthshire or the Water Bailiff. (Machrie 241)

The Tourist Office in Brodick issues a free information sheet showing all the rivers and lochs on the island with charges for fishing.

Arran Angling Association recently stocked Loch Garbad with sizeable brown trout. Daily catch limit is two trout per rod per day. Any river permit also covers permission to fish the loch.

The Iorsa stream is owned by Dougarie Estate. (Machrie 229 or 259)

The Rosa burn is managed by Arran Estates. (Brodick 2203)

SEA ANGLING

Brodick

Arran Sea Angling Centre, The Beach, Brodick. (Brodick 2332) Boats — fishing dinghies with Seagull 40-plus outboards for day or half day. 13-ft dinghies for up to three anglers. Rowing dinghies also available for hire by the hour. Period charter and special rates for club bookings. Rods, reels and tackle for hire or purchase. Bait and freezer facilities.

Lamlash

Johnson's Marine Stores, Old Pier, Lamlash. (Lamlash 333) The island's only marine store and a centre for all marine interests. Comprehensive chandlery stocks.

Lamlash and Kilmory

Neil C. McLean, Torlin Villa, Kilmory. (Sliddery 240). Boats — two by 16-ft longliners, four or five anglers. Bait supplied. Freezer facilities. Accommodation.

Whiting Bay

Stanford Hires, Whiting Bay. (Whiting Bay 313) Boats — 14-ft motorboats. Bait, rods, life jackets etc supplied.

Machrie
Leisure Marine Hire, Machrie. (Machrie 231)
Kildonan
Kildonan Divers, Kildonan Hotel. (Kildonan 207) Boats — four
17-ft Norics with cuddies, one 16½-ft MacKay, 13½-ft Dory, 17-ft
inflatable. Accommodation available — hotel, bunk bed, camping.

Bute

There are some islands off the west coast of Scotland which are
angler's islands and when you visit them with your rod and line
and family (in that order), you get the impression that the people
have *converted* the place to suit ordinary mortals like those who
do not fish. Hoteliers, tourist officers and others seem to have
realised that not everyone fishes. So they bravely offer all sorts of
other amenities and activities to an angler's family. In this
connection bird-watching and wilderness walking and pony
trekking have been manna from Heaven.

The Island of Bute on the Firth of Clyde seems to have worked
all this in reverse. For a century this beautiful island, only a couple
of hour's sailing down the Firth from Glasgow, was the Majorca of
the West of Scotland holiday-makers, and Rothesay its main town
was busy every summer with throngs of trippers, mainly from the
million plus population of the Glasgow industrial area. In a way, it
was to the West of Scotland what Blackpool and Morecambe were
to the mill towns of the North of England or Skegness to the
people of Lincolnshire and Nottinghamshire. It was smaller, of
course, but very, very popular. 'Down the water' was a descriptive
phrase for Father, Mother and the Children going by paddle
steamer down the Clyde and into the Kyles of Bute to disembark
at Rothesay for the Glasgow Fair Fortnight.

Then, of course, along came Spain and packaged holidays and
holiday camps and wider horizons for the Scots and over the years
since the last war the island of Bute, Rothesay in particular,
suffered a serious decline in line with other British seaside places.
Families no longer spent their annual holidays at the Clyde coast
resorts. Business went down and Rothesay became as it once was
— a quiet little seaside town in a pleasant little bay. The
inhabitants too often had the place to themselves, and hotels,
guest houses, restaurants and cafes were left to their depression.

Every year or so there have been signs of a revival. 'Costa Clyde' was a slogan often used to try to motivate investment and renewal. And the people on the island, through their local council, have not lacked vitality or enterprise in trying every scheme possible to get the vacationers back. One side all this *has* been successful for is the conference business. As a venue for meetings, seminars and political rallies, Rothesay has been having its fair share.

The tide is turning in the island's favour. Centred on the famous Winter Garden, there is a spectacular revival in prospect for Rothesay. Financial investment from all sorts of bodies is pouring in.

Although Bute has always had opportunities for visiting anglers, it is only in recent years and in line with the island's renaissance that these have been developed properly. For those who fancy coarse fishing — and let us not forget that these are in the majority in Britain — there is Loch Ascog, a water 1½ miles long containing pike, perch and roach. The pike run from 2lb up to 20lb.

Nearby is the much larger Loch Quien on which boats are available. This is really an excellent trout water and the fish average 1lb. It is three miles from Rothesay on the main road to Kilchatton Bay. Then there is the smaller Loch Fad which has both rainbow and brown trout and is within walking distance of Rothesay. This loch is used as a fish farm by Rothesay Seafood and is therefore kept well stocked.

Sea fishing around Bute is up to the standard of the rest of the Firth of Clyde and attracts anglers from all over the UK. Fishing from the rocky shore or from a boat setting out from Rothesay Pier the prospects of good cod and haddock are always high. The foreshore from Kerrycroy to Kilchatton Bay and Dunagoil are popular spots for shore fishing. The shoreline of Bute consists largely of sand with patches of rubble and stones in parts. Mainly to the south there are short stretches of low rock with sand and shingle bays among them giving concealment to fish.

One of the main factors which made Rothesay famous as a holiday resort is one which also works well today for the sea angler fishing from a boat. The bay is sheltered from the prevailing winds.

Bute is not an island for the angler who is used to the dry-fly purism of the chalkstreams in the south, the long-lining lure fishing of the big English reservoirs, or the thrills of the sea trout as in the Hebrides further north. Still less is he likely to have a rod-bending salmon as a challenge. There are no monster fish out in the Kyles of Bute. In short, Bute is an island for fishing and fun and families. It is the ideal holiday place for the fishing husband who wants to cast a line with his offspring off the shore or even off the pier where some good catches can be made. Alternatively, if he wants the occasional day on a good trout loch with his family with him or not too far away, then this is his place. If he is a coarse fisher so much the better at Loch Ascog, where he may hook a large pike. Getting to Bute is easy from the Glasgow area. There is a roll-on-roll-off ferry from Wemyss Bay and the crossing is thirty minutes.

OTHER ISLANDS IN THE AREA

Cock Island is one of the many islets in the Kyles of Bute and in Loch Fyne. It is just off Tarbert and it has a pretty little plantation of silver birch trees.

Inchmarnock is only forty miles from Glasgow yet very remote. It has no telephone or postal service. It is known as the Calf of Bute, lying just off that main island.

Where To Get Permission To Fish

FRESHWATER FISHING

Loch Fad is seven minutes drive from the centre of Rothesay and is fully stocked with Rainbows by Rothesay Seafood Ltd.

Permits from the Bailiff at the loch or from Bute Tools, 45 Montague Street, Rothesay.

Loch Quien is three miles from Rothesay. Permits from Bute Estate Office, High Street, Rothesay.

Loch Ascog. Coarse fishing. Permits from Bute Estate Office, High Street, Rothesay.

SEA ANGLING

Pier fishing. Permits from the Harbourmaster's Office in the main pier building.

For information about sea fishing cruises and small boats for hire, contact the Isle of Bute Tourist Board at The Pier, Rothesay. (Rothesay 2151)

Charter boats for longer trips from MacLeod Marines, 5-9 Montague Street, Rothesay. (Rothesay 3950) or Mr G. Pellegrotti 27 Bishop Street, Rothesay. (Rothesay 3625)

The Cumbraes

'Get the most of what you want from the most of what you have' That's a saying prevalent these days in one form or another from teachers and those who try to advise others how to live. It is a thought which I would apply to the people on a small island off the west coast of Scotland which, oddly enough, does not have a small name. It is called Great Cumbrae to differentiate it from its adjoining 'calf' island called Little Cumbrae. These Cumbraes Great and Little lie just five minutes sailing on the ferry from the Ayrshire coast at Largs and for years they have been one of the most popular holiday resorts for thousands of families from Glasgow and the rest of industrialised Scotland.

The main town in Great Cumbrae is Millport, a cosy, comfortable, tidy place of neat boarding houses, cafes and a little sandy beach, with a little fun fair and a little of everything to delight children. The island is only four miles by two miles so you might say that Millport *is* Cumbrae.

Apart from its attraction for two hundred years as a place of leisure and holidays, the island does not seem to have blazened its name across the pages of history. Certainly the few inhabitants in the year 1263 must have stood gaping across at the destruction of the biggest Viking fleet of battleships ever to invade Scotland. This armada led by King Haakon of Norway extended from Loch Long in the north right down to the Isle of Arran on the Firth of Clyde. The battle really decided there and then whether Scotland would be Scandinavian or remain Scottish as it is today. The Norsemen had already conquered the Outer Hebrides and much of the north of Scotland. In the King's eyes it seemed a pushover.

The Scots, however, had an army led by King Alexander the Third who put paid to the Norse ambitions. Assisted by a wild storm that day which wrecked many Viking boats, the Scots won the famous Battle of Largs. And among other things the island of Cumbrae was saved by this battle which its inhabitants probably witnessed from only five minutes sail or so across the water.

Even today the general attitude of the people on this little island to the rest of the world is immortalised in the Parish church in Millport, where there is a tombstone erected to the honour of the Reverend James Adam who died in the early nineteenth century. While he was alive as the town's minister, he prayed every

40

Sunday for 'the Great and Little Cumbrae and the adjacent islands of Britain and Ireland'.

The Cumbraes lie downstream of the famous and beautiful Kyles of Bute in the wilder area of the Firth of Clyde. The pastoral tranquillity of Ayrshire with its rich farming land and sandy beaches extends to these islands. Everything is gentle, there are no hills to speak of, no wild crags, no desolate moorlands, nothing to offend the senses all the way round the island from Millport to Millport. Cars are discouraged — they are not much use, anyway — and cycling or walking on the quiet road round the island to visit the delightful little coves and beaches is the best way to enjoy this calm and green little paradise.

For all its apparent insignificance on the pages of history, the Cumbraes have had a role to play in the introduction of Christianity to Scotland. The earliest village was at Kirkton, about half a mile from Millport, where there is a chapel 'Cumbrayne' dedicated in 1330 to St. Columba who had founded the important religious settlement on Iona, another island further north.

The past fifty years have given Millport an ebb and flow of summer holiday visitors from mainland Scotland and elsewhere. Today there is a revival and almost every amusement, sport and activity is available on the island — sailing, swimming, golf, bowling, tennis, pony and horse riding, cycling, game fishing on the only two adjoining reservoirs and, of course, sea angling from the rocks or by boat from the harbour. And there are discos, dances and cabarets galore.

Great Cumbrae has become great in its own right — not by size but by the enterprise and hard work of the island's inhabitants.

Fishing on Great Cumbrae

There are two opportunities for anglers on the island. First there is the trout fishing available to visitors (four tickets per day only) by courtesy of the small but energetic local angling club. This club has thirty members and leases the two adjoining local reservoirs from Bute Estates. They stock them with about a thousand brown trout in one and the same number of rainbows in the second.

Fishing is by fly only, of course, and the day's catch limit is six fish per angler. In a year about 200 fish are caught of a weight

FISHING THE SCOTTISH ISLANDS

between 1 and 4lb. Permits can be obtained at a very moderate price on a daily or weekly basis from the local tobacconist shop in the town.

The other opportunity is for sea angling. Boats can be hired from Millport harbour. Those who fancy going further afield after the big cod can join a party on one of the charter trips that go out frequently. The Firth of Clyde is renowned for its big catches and Millport is well situated for reaching the hot spots.

Where to get Permission to Fish

FRESHWATER FISHING

Trout fishing on two reservoirs. Contact Mrs B. Hill, Tobacconist, Stuart Street, Millport.

SEA ANGLING

Good fishing from various points along the rocky shore. Two boats may be available for charter from F.V.G. Mapes and Son, 3 Guildford Street, Millport.

Gigha

Sea anglers will probably hate me for telling this tale. But first, for those who have never gone out on the ocean waves in a boat sea fishing, let me explain what happens.

First, there's the getting ready. You and others in your club sort out your rods and reels and hooks and spinners in the garage *days* before you go. You meet each other and discuss intricate matters like whether you will use ragworm for bait or rubber eels or riggers or wobblers or up-and-downers or sideways plonkers. Things like paternoster rigs and three-ounce triangular lead weights and mussel and cockle 'cocktails' are matters of serious planning. How to prevent over-spin on your multiplier reel is every bit as important as tide-drift and wind direction.

That is what you do days before you even *get* to the sea.

Then the skipper of your chartered boat takes you and your friends two or three miles out to what are called 'marks' — these are the places where he knows and you know there are plenty of fish. Huge cod and big ling and enormous conger eels are just waiting for these rods and lines to send down their lunch.

If nothing happens after two hours you don't have to look far for expert advice, because *all* sea anglers are experts on everything from down-tide floaters to mackerel strips on No. 6 hooks. So there is a lot of talk about what may be wrong usually ending up with a request to the skipper to up-anchor and head for another mark two miles out. So he knocks out his pipe, folds up his newspaper and starts up the engine. Then the while rigmarole starts up again.

In a way, salmon and trout anglers are not very much different. If anything, we are *worse* with our worries about fishing flies and sink-and-draw methods and upstream nymphing and all sorts of mythology. It is little wonder that most fish have a permanent grin on their faces.

The reason I am writing all this is that the one and only time I visited the island of Gigha off the Mull of Kintyre was when I was with a BBC team recording some of the people there and I was hunting around for some news about the fishing opportunities. And if any of my sea-fishing friends had been with me that day they might have thrown away all their rods and reels and all their gear.

At that time the one and only trout loch on the island — the Mill Loch — was almost troutless. Some years of neglect had surrendered this water to the resident pike and other coarse fish. The situation is very different today, of course, but of that — more later.

It took me an hour or so to hunt down Gigha's best-known fisherman — Hamish McKenzie — whose cottage was just up and along from the landing pier. I told him that I was looking for information about angling opportunities on Gigha and he suggested the sea. He said he was going out in his small boat that afternoon to catch some mackerel for bait for his lobster pots but if I wanted to come with him, I would be welcome. Since there seemed no other opportunity for casting a line, I thanked him and arranged to meet him at the jetty with my gear.

So there we were, out in his boat and there was I sitting in the bow with my expensive rod and multiplier reel and surrounded with plinkers and plonkers of all shapes and sizes. Hamish was sitting in the stern with nothing except a long, straight pole. No reel, no line — nothing.

'Where's your rod, Hamish,' I said.

'Here,' he said, nodding to this thing which I now recognised as a well-worn broom handle.

'For catching fish?'

'Oh, yes. For the saith and the mackerel.'

'There's no reel.'

'Och, I can't be bothered with these things.'

'And where's the line?'

'Man, it's on the end of it — that wee bit of string.'

Then I noticed there *was* a length of string at the top of the broom handle and it ran down the side of it. On it were half-a-dozen hooks with little coloured elastic bands straggled all over them. Elastic bands!

When we started fishing I thought I was dreaming. There I was with all this fancy tackle of mine pulling up an odd bewildered little fish. And there was Hamish hoisting that silly old broom handle over the end of the boat and jiggling these hooks up and down, then pulling up the string with *six* big fish at a time.

When we were sitting in front of his cottage later having a dram together, he said, 'Och, man, I wouldn't have any time for this angling nonsense. It's too slow — getting one little fish at a time. No, no. That wouldn't do me at all — nor would it fill my lobster creels.'

When I got back home from that trip I thought of selling all my sea angling equipment and buying myself a broom handle and six hooks with coloured elastic bands.

More seriously, the situation today for anglers on Gigha has changed very much for the better. I am not sure if Hamish still has his broom handle and elastic bands for catching mackerel, or even if he still has his lobster pots. What I *do* know is that the Mill Loch is now an excellent brown and rainbow trout water. The pike have gone and it is an excellent fishing spot on a lovely, remote island. The loch is stocked every two years and cared for by the island's only hotel where permission to fish can be obtained.

Where to get Permission to Fish

FRESHWATER FISHING

Permission to fish the Mill Loch is available to guests of the Gigha Hotel. (Gigha 254)

SEA ANGLING

Although there are no organised charterers or boat hirers, one of the local lobster fishermen will no doubt be pleased to accommodate a visiting angler for offshore fishing.

Islay

I can never understand why the Celts decided to use the Gaelic word for a 'boy' to describe a ghillie. Nearly all the ghillies *I've* ever had with me on a salmon river or out on a loch have looked at least a hundred years old, had faces like hewn granite, grey hair sprouting out everywhere and had every quality under the sun opposite to that associated with a 'boy'.

A ghillie on a river is a know-all — and I don't mean that disparagingly. He usually *does* know it all — which pools to fish, where the salmon are lying, what flies to use. Then he'll tell you where to cast your fly, how to retrieve it on the edge of the white water, what to do if the fish takes your fly and he'll land it with a tailer or a net as neat as you like. He is an artist.

It's their *patience* I admire. Can you imagine what it must be like to have been fishing all your life, caught hundreds of salmon or trout, then sit on a river bank all day while some idiot wallops a rod all over the place, scares the daylights out of every fish for miles around then gets his salmon fly hooked up on a tree on the other side of the river, and asks you if you can get it off for him?

I am not denying *I* have been one of these idiots. I don't feel so daft now when I am with a ghillie because there *are* a few notches on the butt of my fishing rod, but I can well remember the first time I had a ghillie with me on a salmon river.

Johnnie MacFadzen was the first ghillie I ever met in my life, though he was not the last. They're a very exceptional kind of people. You usually find that their fathers and grandfathers were ghillies before them — usually on that same river in the days when His Lordship owned the estate and a day on the river with a ghillie was an experience of a lifetime. Certainly that day with Johnnie on a Highland salmon river was one I will remember all my life — for reasons other than the fishing.

'Ye'll be wantin' a dram with your lunch, sir?' he said as we were putting our things in the car.

'A dram? Yes. Should I get a bottle of whisky from the hotel?'

'Ye'll do nothing of the kind! That blended stuff — *that's* not for a day on the river. I'll bring one along.'

The bottle he brought had no label. And the liquid inside had no colouring — I thought it was water. And before we had our lunch, there we were sitting on the river-bank in the sunshine beside that sparkling, gurgling, white-foamed salmon pool as he poured out for me a glass of the most magnificent single-malt whisky I had ever tasted in my life.

After the first sip, I said, '*That* is a whisky and a half!'

'It is. It is that.'

'I see the bottle has no label. You're not telling me that you made it yourself, are you?'

He looked at me sideways. 'Now why would I be doin' that — even if I *did* know how to make it — when I have a brother who's in a distillery?'

I took another mouthful of the delectable liquid. 'Around here?'

He shook his head. 'Not here. It's where they make the best whisky in the world.'

'That'll be Speyside.'

He shook his head, enjoying teasing me.

'Aberdeenshire?'

He continued shaking his head.

'I give up. Where?'

He sucked his lips over his next sip. 'It's an *Islay* malt.'

'And that's where your brother works?'

He nodded and I said no more. I determined there and then to visit this Treasure Island called Islay off the western seaboard of Scotland where they make such a drink of the gods. I had to wait another seven years before I got the opportunity. I was on my way through to Jura — only a narrow sound away — and I stopped over on this most southerly of the Hebridean islands (indeed the island is more southerly than Glasgow or Edinburgh). I *did* sample the whisky, and at the first sip all the wonderful memories of that day by the river with the brother of the man who made it (I had felt sure he *must* have made it himself) came flooding back to me.

I found out a lot about both the whisky and the fishing on Islay while I was there. There are eight distilleries on the island making the smoky-flavoured nectar which is an ingredient of nearly every blended Scotch whisky on the market today. But as single malts, many of them stay and are sold on the island — the inhabitants know a good thing! The oldest distillery is Bowmore which was established in 1779 and is still privately owned making a famous 12-year-old single malt spirit. All of the others, with one exception, were started at various stages in the nineteenth century when there was a great upsurge in demand for whisky in Britain and elsewhere in the world.

Probably the best-known Islay whisky is Laphroaig. The distillery which makes this nectar dates back to 1815 and the malting floor today is traditional as are the pagoda chimneys outside. This whisky has such a distinctive peaty-smoky flavour that it can be recognised instantly on the first sip.

Somehow in Scotland there always seems to be a relationship between a good dram and good fishing. Sometimes the best fishing is to be found where they make the best whisky. Sometimes it is simply a poetic matter where no day's angling is complete without a dram at lunchtime. Sometimes it is simply a matter of using one to toast the other. And the relationship seems to me to be at the heart of Islay's attraction.

In general terms the visiting angler would be well advised to think twice about salmon or even sea trout fishing, since all of it is preserved although *some* access is available through the hotels. Another thing he should do is pray for rain because the three rivers depend almost entirely on spates — the Sorn in the centre of the island, the Laggan in the north-east arm and a little river with an unpronounceable Gaelic name called in English the Blackwater. These rivers are usually booked year after year at the best times of the season by the same tenants. Indeed, while I was gathering material for this book, a lady with a lovely Highland voice telephoned me urgently to say that 'her' river (one of the three mentioned above) was *not* available for visitors as the same people came year after year to fish it and would I please not mention it.

The Sorn river is sourced at Loch Finlaggan and you might think that salmon would ascend the river and be fished for in the loch. Yet there is record of only one salmon being caught. This was in 1930 and the man who caught it was Sir Harry Lauder the world-famous Scots comedian and singer. It is for trout that anglers fish Loch Finlaggan which is ten miles from Bowmore and about three miles south-west of the village of Port Askaig. There are islands scattered round the loch and it is around these that the best catches can be made. Finlaggan Castle is on one of the islands and it adds a charm and a drama to the water.

Ballygrant is another trout loch a few miles away from Finlaggan and can be fished either from bank or boat. A wind to ripple the water is essential for good trouting here.

Like the fishing on most of the Hebridean islands, it is the hotels which have the access and facilities for lochs such as Gorm, Lossit, Solon, Glencastle and Allan because they have arrangements with the estates. The estates with salmon fishing are Dunlossit, Islay and Laggan. Loch Gorm is the largest loch on the island. It is nine miles from Bridgend where the hotel issues permits as well as those for four other lochs. There are six boats in all. River fishing for salmon and sea trout sometimes *can* be arranged if there are vacancies, although the real limiting factor here is simply the rainfall.

Spates or not, it is interesting to note that the River Laggan which has the best salmon fishing in its lower four miles has been producing 300 fish in a season.

Islay Estate has ten trout lochs, the main ones being Gorm, Skerrols and Finlaggan. Lochs Laingaedil, Drolsay, Cam and Smigeadail are further afield and entail some stiff walking but like most remote lochs are very rewarding in terms of exclusiveness and the prospect of 'uneducated' trout. Permits for all these lochs on Islay are very cheap.

What about the sea anglers who might want to haul aboard a huge conger or a record skate? Sea fishing opportunities are many and Port Ellen and Port Askaig have good harbours. Cod, haddock, whiting, coalfish, pollack, mackerel, gurnard, dogfish, spurdog, plaice, flounder, tope, ling, conger, skate and rays are possible catches, and Port Charlotte Hotel has a twenty-foot boat.

How to get to Islay? The fastest and most convenient way, of course, is by air from Glasgow or Edinburgh although it is also the most expensive. And there is always the question of a car once you are on the island, although hiring facilities are quite plentiful.

The other way is by car ferry run by Caledonian MacBrayne from Kennacraig in West Loch Tarbert to either Port Ellen or Port Askaig. This takes about 2 hours, but then there is also the long drive around the indented bays and sounds via Inveraray and Lochgilphead. Little wonder that air travel is so popular!

OTHER ISLANDS IN THE AREA

Am Fraoch Eilean is just off the southern shore in the Sound of Islay. There are ruins of a castle built to Somerled, King of Argyll in the twelfth century. It was hoped that it would guard the Sound against Norse invaders.

Council Island is really an islet and it lies in Loch Finlaggan on Islay. It was the place where the fourteen clan chiefs met to advise the Lord of the Isles.

Where to get Permission to Fish

FRESHWATER FISHING

Bridgend

Bridgend Hotel has fishing on five lochs including the famous Loch Gorm. Contact Mr Wiles, the Head Keeper (049 681 293) who can also arrange salmon and sea trout fishing on Islay Estates which has ten good trout lochs, four with boats. Also contact the Estate Office, Islay House. (Bowmore 293)

Port Askaig

Guests at the Port Askaig Hotel can obtain fishing for trout on many local lochs — also for salmon on the River Laggan. Tickets for these and other lochs can also be obtained from the Port Askaig Shop. (Port Askaig 663)

Port Charlotte

Guests at the Port Charlotte Hotel can have fishing on six lochs including Loch Gorm.

Port Ellen

Guests at Machriue Hotel can have brown trout fishing on Lochs Gorm, Ballygrant, Lossit, Finlaggan, Solon (which also has salmon and sea trout) and Glencastle by arrangement with keepers. Trout fishing can also be arranged by contacting Mr V. Montgomery, Kinebus Farm, The Oa, Port Ellen. (Port Ellen 2366)

SEA ANGLING

Any of the hotels mentioned above can arrange for sea fishing trips for guests by arranging local charters or hires of small craft.

Jura

'I don't need fishing all *that* much,' I said to the gamekeeper.

He sat back in his ingle-nook in the hotel bar and laughed, 'Och, but you'll not be letting a little walk stop you from catching a trout or two.'

'A *little* walk?'

Nothing is easy or comfortable for the angler on the Isle of Jura — except, of course, the hotel. The salmon fishing is private and tied to the self-catering cottages by the river Lussa and, like that of most Hebridean islands, is entirely dependent on rain for its productivity of fish. The Lussa is a spate river and a visiting angler can find himself in a Catch 22 situation. It runs like this — the guests in the estate cottages have the first rights to the river, so booking well in advance is advised. But — and here is the dilemma — booking months in advance means booking 'blind' and there may be no rain. No rain — no salmon. No salmon — no fishing.

This is why on an island like Jura the best bet for a visitor with a fishing rod is on one of the forty lochs. Ardlussa Estate has some good hill lochs for the trout fisher and the hotel, of course, can also arrange fishing on many of the other lochs. But — and here is the other discomfort — almost all of them entail considerable walking on very rough ground in *very* wild country. Jura is no place for the angler who insists on minimum effort in getting his sport. There are only a few miles of road and the rest of the island has hardly a track.

For those who *do* like their hill walking and a sense of exploration with their trout fishing, however, Jura is filled with evidence of ancient history, tradition, legend and incredible wild beauty. It is reckoned that it has been inhabited for about 5,000 years — from the early Bronze age through the Viking period to the days of warfare among the clans — mainly the MacDonalds and the Campbells. The Standing Stones, such as those on the Camus Stack which are twelve feet high and four feet across, are reputed to have been erected before the Pyramids in Egypt. There are also remains of hill forts and two ruined castles.

For those who like to look at graveyards when they are away from their fishing, the one at Inverlussa has some interesting indicators to the past. St. Columba, who is said to have brought

Christianity to mainland Britain when he settled on Iona and formed a church there, had close contact with Jura; his uncle St. Earnan is buried here. There is also the grave of a woman, Mary McCrain, who lived for 128 years. One of her ancestors, Gilbert McCrain who died in the twelfth century, is said to have lived for 180 years. That must say something for the healthy air of Jura!

The island is thirty miles long and seven miles wide and although it is third largest island in Argyll it is the most remote and least known. The population is less than 250 and there are just sufficient visitors and tourists to prevent the complete isolation of the inhabitants. The part of the island which is the seaboard, all along the northwest, is one of the wildest and starkest in Britain. There are no roads here and the only access to the beaches and cliffs and caves is by boat.

The sea angling potential for anyone brave enough to cast a line off this northwest coast is tremendous. 'Brave' is the correct word here because to the north is the notorious Gulf of Corryvreckan, which even today is deemed by the Royal Navy to be unnavigable. The gulf is only a mile across and the sound about two miles long, but it is here that a whirlpool is formed at certain times of the tide when there is a strong westerly wind. Currents from the mainland meet those from the ocean in the narrow strait between Jura and the Island of Scarba. When this happens the fearsome maelstrom can be seen from the shore. It was once described by an early scribe as 'a conflux so dreadful that it spurns all description. At the distance of twelve miles a most dreadful noise as if all the infernal powers had been let loose is heard . . . and an eddy is formed which would swallow up the largest ship of the line.'

They say that when Corryvreckan is asleep, when the tide is right and there is no strong westerly wind, a small boat can pass without harm. For my part, I would certainly never attempt a sea angling trip near that slumbering monster.

Deer stalking (the name Jura means Deer) and grouse shooting are in great demand on the estates and it is in the autumn, prime season for these sports, that fishing is limited for reasons of safety. However, before this and during the summer there are all sorts of activities available for non-anglers from the hotel — exploring with the guidance of local fishermen and stalkers, visits to the local whisky distillery, pony trekking, bird-watching (there are over a hundred species of birds) or bathing on any of the splendid beaches.

Many of the visitors who come to Jura have a great interest in George Orwell, the author of *Nineteen Eighty-Four* among many other books. He came from London to live on Jura in 1946, in a remote farmhouse called Barnhill in the north of the island, where he started farming and gardening in a small way. He said he was 'anxious to get out of London for my own sake because I am constantly smothered under journalism. I want to write another book which is impossible unless I get six months quiet . . . somewhere where I cannot be telephoned to.' Up until then, Orwell had written a few books and was working as a journalist for various newspapers, mainly *The Observer*. It was while he was on Jura that his tuberculosis became critical, and he died later in a hospital in the south.

It was while I was on Jura with a BBC Radio team that we met and taped Mrs Nelson of Ardlussa who was Orwell's next door neighbour, although their houses were six miles apart. In a sense she was the nearest link the author had with the outside world. There is a fascinating little booklet *Jura and George Orwell* available from the Jura Hotel and it contains Mrs Nelson's reminiscences of the author.

I have often felt it quite surprising why the smallest and often the most trivial detail stays in the memory after an experience like the one we had on Jura that day. The estate gamekeeper drove me round a good part of the island, showed me the salmon river and some of the other waters, I asked him about the pattern of flies to be used on the lochs.

'Oh, just about any of the good old standbys,' he said. 'You know — Soldier Palmer, Grouse and Claret or Greenwells. Except on the tail.'

'What d'you use on the tail?'

'A Blue Zulu.'

'But that's a sea trout fly.'

'Well, maybe. But *that's* what we use on Jura for the brown trout. *And* it catches, believe me!'

Where to get Permission to Fish
FRESHWATER FISHING

The main river on Jura is the Lussa and enquiries about fishing should be made to Mr C. Fletcher, Ardlussa Estate, Ardlussa, Jura. (049682 323)

The other source of information and for obtaining permits is the Jura Hotel, Isle of Jura, Argyll PA60 7XU (Jura 243)

SEA ANGLING

Fishing from the rocks and shores around the island — or from a dinghy. Advice and boat hire for guests of the Jura Hotel.

Colonsay

Not every angler wants to catch salmon, wants huge baskets of trout, desires intense competition with other anglers, wants expensive beats on famous fishing rivers or even needs the stimulation of fishing with others.

There is an island in the Inner Hebrides in Scotland which I feel sure was made by nature for the 'other' kind of angler and for families who want above anything the beauty and serenity of calm lochs and golden shores where the size of a day's catch comes very much second to everything else.

If I were looking for a place to have a family holiday with a little fishing thrown in and long, wonderful summer days of tranquility in a place only 2½ hours sailing from the Scottish mainland at Oban, I would plump for the island of Colonsay. It lies twenty-five miles to the south of Mull and like its neighbours Coll and Tiree benefits from the warm climate of the Gulf Stream. There are over 150 species of birds and over 500 different types of flora recorded on this island and seals and otters are fairly common.

Colonsay is a kind of dream-island for anyone on vacation, whether they fish or not. Once there were three islands, Colonsay being split in two by the then water-filled Kiloran Glen. Now there are two — well, for much of the day at any rate. The tides have the last say on the matter between Colonsay and the small Oronsay just off the south shore. And at low tide it is possible to walk from one to the other.

Although there is a car ferry from Oban to the small harbour of Scalasaig on Colonsay, it is not primarily intended for tourist use. Anyway, it is doubtful if a car can be all that useful on an island that only has about thirteen miles of useable road for cars. And, of course, the island itself is only 8½ miles long and about three miles wide. For all this, it *does* have an eight-hole golf course!

For anglers there are three lochs. It depends whom you ask or what guidebooks you read as to the size or number of trout you may expect to catch on each of them. Certainly the best-known loch is Fada. This is a long, narrow loch of three separate waters and the trout here, by all accounts, come out just under a pound. Because of weed-growth in summer, fishing from a boat is advised and one can be hired from the Isle of Colonsay Hotel.

A little hill dam especially made by one of the laird's ancestors for fishing is Loch Tuirmain which produces ¾-pound trout — fishing only from the bank. The third one is Loch Sgoltaire which lies near Kiloran. This is the laird's own loch and although I have never fished it myself, Moray McLaren and W. B. Currie in their book *The Fishing Waters of Scotland* really surprised me by their enthusiastic description. They say that the loch ' . . . is a charming round hill loch with a quaint little arbour on an island. You could fish it all day and hardly touch a trout, but suddenly you would be playing a fish of two or three pounds. Scoulter (as they name it) trout are very big and have run to several pounds — six, seven, even eight . . .'

There are some sea trout on Colonsay. They feed in and out of the sandy bays where the small burns enter the ocean.

For vacationers who do not fish, Colonsay has everything for a peaceful and memorable holiday. There are the magnificent, blue-hazed views of the nearby islands of Mull, Jura and Islay, of course, but the exotic Kiloran Gardens are reckoned to be among the most beautiful in Scotland. On the west coast there is splendid cliff scenery where countless seabirds of all types breed. On Oronsay, hundreds of barnacle geese winter and just off the southern point there are many seals to be seen.

The fishing on Colonsay is free to guests of both the hotel and of the cottages and guest houses.

Where to get permission to fish
FRESHWATER FISHING
Fishing on three lochs on the island is free to residents of the Colonsay Hotel. (Colonsay 316)

Mull
Salmon reared in fish farms . . . lochs and reservoirs stocked with pellet-fed rainbow and brown trout . . .. Is the sea around the British coasts now the only water wilderness? Where *are* the wild fish?

I can tell you where there are thousands of them — in the fresh waters of Mull.

The Prince of freshwater game fish so far to defy the fish ranchers or the stewponds is the sea trout. This is the silver darling of sports fishers who search the world every summer for what they believe is the greatest angling challenge of all. And their sea trout safaris to Scotland take them to the Ythan at Newburgh, to the Eichaig near Dunoon and to the Border Esk at Canonbie, rivers now more renowned for sea trout than for salmon. Their annual fishing trips ought also to take them to the sea trout Valhallas of the Aberdeenshire Ugie or the Deveron, to the North and South Esks in Angus or the Nith in Dumfriesshire where six thousand sea trout were caught by anglers in 1988!

Now I have something to add to their adventures — the island of Mull.

The sea trout is the most obliging of fish — and this is particularly true in Mull — because it times its spawning run to suit the summer holiday angler. Mull sea trout do not usually come into the rivers and lochs until the middle of June, although prior to this they may be caught from the shore where there is an outflow of fresh water. From June onward, providing there is plenty of rain, the fishing can be very good and entirely concurrent with the visit of summer tourists.

First the sea trout rivers.

The Forsa flows into the Sound of Mull a short distance from Salen on the west coast. As well as being the island's best salmon river (forty good holding pools) it has good runs of sea trout from late June. The river is divided into six beats and they rotate. The local hotel and the tackle shop in Tobermory sell permits.

The Bellart has three miles available to visitors. Much depends on rainfall and the tide conditions and if these are right, good catches can be made. Finnock run into the river from as early as May. Another small but good sea trout river is the Coladoir. Like the Bellart, it is on the west side of the island.

The Aros, a very popular sea trout river is 5½ miles long. Conversely, the Ba is a very short river which runs from Loch Ba to the sea, a distance of only 2½ miles. The sea pools on this river are available to visitors but other parts and the loch fishing are only occasionally available on application to Killichronan

Estates. Plopping fish at the mouth of the Ba have often fooled anglers but they are usually grey mullet and almost impossible to catch.

The Forestry Commission has a stretch of the River Lussa for which permits can be obtained at the Commission's premises in Glen Aros.

Of course, all these rivers also produce salmon.

There are some anglers who swear that no sport on earth can match fishing for sea trout on a loch. Whether wet-fly fishing or dapping, the thrill of a good-sized sea trout snatching the fly is a tremendous experience. And Mull has its share of lochs with such a potential

Loch Tor has a run of sea trout as well as the resident brownies. The occasional sea trout and salmon can be taken on Mull's largest loch — Loch Frisa. Incidentally, Mull's largest salmon — a fish of 45lb — was caught here in 1911 by Mr. James Greenhill from Edinburgh.

Down in the Ross of Mull, the largest loch is Loch Assapol which contains brown trout and has its run of sea trout, including the largest so far caught — a fish of 7½lb. Over to the west is Loch Sguabain which is also a good sea trout water. The English translation of this loch's name is 'windswept' which speaks for itself, as there is always a good breeze providing excellent drifts for a boat. Because the loch has dense weed in parts, dapping or dry-fly fishing is recommended. In 1984 David Howitt, a well-known local angler and author, caught a sea trout of 9½lb on a silver 'Krill'. This same angler, incidentally, while fishing with the late Alisdair Cattanach on Loch Uisg caught fourteen sea trout in one afternoon in 1977 by dapping. The biggest was 4lb. This loch has a shoreline of four miles. Loch Ba, from which the river of the same name runs, has a shoreline of eight miles and is therefore usually fished from a boat. Dapping is popular early in the season and although spinning with a Toby later is practised, wet-fly fishing is the more satisfying method for the sea trout. The late Alisdair Cattanach in October 1978 landed an 9½lb sea trout using a cast of only 6lb.

Rivers and lochs apart, there is another prospect for sea trout fishing on Mull and that is the shoreline of which there are 300 miles, with thousands of fishing marks. From May to July shoals of the fish gather in the shallow waters near the estuary of small streams. Spinning is the best method here but when there is an offshore wind the wet-fly can be very productive.

With such a long shoreline around the island, it would be surprising if the opportunities for sea fishing were not great. And this is indeed the case. There is such a variety of venues — from sandy beaches of Calgary — to other areas further west where it is possible to drop hook and bait directly into twenty fathoms of water. In the sandy regions there are codling, flatfish and rays while on the rocky grounds there are pollack, coalfish, wrasse, conger and dogfish.

Sea fishing charter trips and the hire of smaller craft are readily available from Tobermory and Dervaig. Let no sea angler forget that ten Scottish fishing records have so far been broken at Tobermory.

How to get to this fishing Elysium? It is all much simpler, easier and quicker than the journey to many other of the Western Hebrides, particularly Lewis or Harris. There are regular car ferries from Oban taking only forty minutes and from Loch Aline taking even shorter — fifteen minutes. There is also a passenger service from Kilchoan and there is a small airfield at Connel near Oban which can accept suitable charter flights.

Slip from Grace on Mull

For an angler nearly every island around Scotland has a snag — sometimes big, sometimes small. Some Hebridean islands have excellent and easily accessible trout fishing but offer little to the salmon or sea trout fisher. Others do have good salmon runs but the charges are high, permission difficult to obtain, and some island waters are ill-managed and poached to despair. What a joy it is to find an island where the fishing is well managed, the charges reasonable and the choice of lochs or rivers wide and tempting!

I first fell in love with Mull during a three-week holiday with my family some years ago. We rented a cottage in Tobermory and I was granted full permission to fish every second day. Of course, the first place I visited was the fishing tackle shop in the town. The man who served me was the answer to an angler's prayer. After I had purchased some flies and some odds and ends, he said, 'Are you fishing on your own?'

'Yes. My family's here but they don't fish.'

'Maybe you could do with a companion.'

I was cautious. 'Well — maybe.'

'Why don't you go round the corner to this address' — he wrote a street and a number on a piece of paper — 'and say I sent you.'

'Hughie McCall,' I read. 'Is he a ghillie?'

'He's better than that. He's a retired gamekeeper. Been retired for a few years. He has a big reputation here but I think he'd appreciate a day or so fishing. Y'see, he's got no car and getting to the waters is too far by walking.'

'Right. I'll give him a call.'

I did. And our relationship was the experience of a lifetime. Hughie was over seventy, grey-haired, twinkle-eyed and he spoke both Gaelic and English. He swore in Gaelic when he missed a fish and spoke politely in English otherwise. He had many other things — a sense of humour, tremendous patience, a taste for a dram and, most importantly, a vast knowledge of the island's fishing waters, many of old which he had been guardian of for the riparian owners.

He was grateful for my offer to take him fishing. Take him fishing? Apart from my contribution in terms of buying the permits, driving the car and supplying the lunch and the odd dram, Hughie took *me* on some of the finest outings I had ever had with rod and line.

The funny thing about gamekeepers is that they don't seem to have changed much over the past hundred years. You can still turn up the pages of old magazines like *Punch* and see the ruddy-faced, brawny bailiff with his leggings and tweed jacket and fore-and-aft tweed hat — a formidable foe, a policeman in a checked suit whose by-word to the poacher by the river-side is 'Gotcher!'

Gamekeepers on fishing rivers keep the poachers off, of course — that is one of their main jobs — but they are a lot more than river-watchers. A gamekeeper is an expert. He knows where the fish are; he can tell you exactly where to cast your fly and he will help you net the fish if you are lucky. He knows all about double-haul casting and floating lines and upstream dry-flying and all the flies that the fish will go for on that river. He will pick a Munro Killer or a Golden Butcher or a Murray's Bluebottle Spider out of your fly-box and say, '*That's* the wee boy for a day like this. Tie that one on.' And — sure as fate — that is usually the wee boy that catches them.

There is another thing that a gamekeeper knows like the back of his hand — how to tie knots. If he says you need a double-blood knot on your tail-fly, you would be daft to tie anything else. Gamekeepers know the game.

Hughie McCall's reputation as an angling expert around Tobermory was something like that of a Japanese Samurai Warrior. What he did not know about salmon or trout fishing wasn't worth knowing. And he was proud of his reputation. In a pub in Tobermory, if anybody raised the subject of fishing, the place went as quiet as a grave until everyone listened to what Hughie had to say.

We started off with the Mishnish Lochs — these are the ones nearest Tobermory and they are stocked regularly with brown trout by the local angling club. Hughie caught our first — a trout of 1½lb — on an ever-faithfull Greenwell's Glory as the tail fly. Then I caught my share — three fish all under a pound.

We were off. Every other day we fished one or other of Mull's splendid waters — Loch Tor which is stocked with Rainbows, Loch Frisa which is the island's largest loch, Aros Loch where the trout sulk in the deep, dark places. Then one rainy day Hughie decided it was time for us to join the big league and he suggested the River Aros. He told me where to buy the permits and off we went.

I stopped the car up on a high bank along a single-track road beside the river. The water was running coffee-coloured in its dying spate.

'Wid ye look at that river!' Hughie said.

'And it's starting to run off,' I said.

We were out of the car and setting up our rods in an instant. Hughie was bright-eyed and straining to contain his enthusiasm.

'What fly?' I asked as I held out my fly-box for him to make the selection.

'*That's* him,' he pointed a work-hardened forefinger at a double-hooked fly. 'The Blue Charm. Deadly.'

'You're sure?'

He gave me a destructive look. 'I'm certain.'

I felt so ashamed at doubting his judgement that I willingly let him tie the fly on to my nylon cast.

He tied the fly on with one of his never-fail knots and when he had finished there was a scraggy end of nylon sticking out.

'Now, d'you see that? *That* can put the salmon off — just at the last minnit when he's about to take the fly. Where's your scissors?' He snipped the end of it and — I'll tell you the truth — I had the feeling that he had cut it too short. So I said so.

'Short?' He looked at me from under his craggy eyebrows. '*Short?* Ye're telling me how to tie a salmon fly?'

'No, no, Hughie. I'd never dream of it. But supposing the fish works that knot loose.'

He just laughed and patted me on the shoulder. 'Jist you cast that fly in the river and let the salmon worry about that. With Hughie McCall's knots, once a salmon's hooked — he *stays* hooked.'

Even now, I hardly know how to say this. I was fishing the first pool, Hughie the second. Within twenty minutes I was into a big fish. And within twenty-three minutes he was off. I could hardly believe it as I reeled in a sickening limp line. And the fly at the end was gone.

I was speechless when Hughie came up to me. 'It *couldn't* be the knot,' he said. 'It's your nylon. It must have been weak or frayed or something. The knot? It's impossible.'

I didn't say a word. I just showed him the end of the line and there it was for anyone to see — a spiral of nylon proving beyond doubt that the fish had worked that knot loose.

I never saw a fellow-angler so shattered in all my life. All the way back to Tobermory he didn't say a word. Then when we got to his home, he said in a slightly-broken voice, 'I'd be obliged if we kept this sad day to ourselves.'

And I did — until now. Hughie passed away last year.

OTHER ISLANDS IN THE AREA

Eileach an naoimh is the 'island of the saints' and is the most southerly of a chain of very small uninhabited island called the Gravellachs. It is one of the earliest Christian settlements in the Western Isles and has the reputed grave of St Ethane, mother of Columba. It is said that this island was Columba's favourite retreat from Iona which is thirty-odd miles to the west.

Erraid is another tiny island — one square mile — and it lies so close to the shore in the Sound of Iona that you can walk across to Mull at low tide. Robert Louis Stevenson's father, who was an engineer, used it as a base camp for the building of Skerryvore and Dubh Heartach lighthouses.

Iona is famous throughout the world as the cradle of Christianity in Scotland. The religious settlement was founded here by Columba in 563. In 1899 the ruins of the abbey were gifted to the Church of Scotland. Then in 1938 a team of six craftsmen and six ministers, inspired by the ideas of a visionary minister from Govan, Glasgow, the Reverend George MacLeod, began to restore the abbey ruins. Today thousands of visitors visit the Iona Community travelling by the short ferry crossing at the southern tip of Mull.

Inch Kenneth sits less than a mile off the shores of Mull. It is named after one of Columba's colleagues. Many clan chiefs were buried here when the crossing to Iona was too stormy.

Staffa. With its magnificent basalt columns, hexagonal and regular, the island of Staffa seven miles west of Mull is one of Britain's geological treasures, encompassing Fingal's Cave which was the inspiration in 1829 of Mendelssohn's Hebridean Overture.

The cave was first discovered in 1772 by Sir Joseph Banks who had previously been with Captain Cook on his 1768 exploration of the South Seas.

Since then many famous authors, poets and composers have visited the island and expressed their feelings about it — Sir Walter Scott, Jules Verne, Wordsworth, Keats, Tennyson, and painters such as Turner. Queen Victoria and the royal family visited it in 1847.

Incidentally, in 1800 the price of an excursion to the island was two bottles of whisky and fifteen shillings!

The Treshnish Isles are a group of islands west of Mull and south-east of Coll. They are very rich in bird life and are a breeding ground for the grey seal.

Ulva is an island off the west coast of Mull. The ownership of this island is said to have been with the clan MacQuarrie for 900 years. Many of the MacArthurs, who were famed as pipers throughout the isles, ran their college of piping on this island.

Other islands around or in the direction of Mull are Dubh Artaech, Eorsa, Fladda and Little Colonsay.

Where to get Permission to Fish

FRESHWATER FISHING

River Aros

Fishing permits available from Captain D. Scott, Glenaros, Mull. (06803 337)

River Ba

Permits from Killichronan Estates. (06803 438)

River Bellart

Permits available from Tackle and Books, Tobermory (0688 2336) or Dick Fairbairns. (Dervaig 275)

River Coladoir

Permits from Sandy Peddie, Rossal. (06814 210)

River Forsa

Permits from Glenforsa Hotel, (06803 377) Tackle and Books, Tobermory. (0688 2336) Mull Travel and Crafts, Craignure. (06802 487)

River Lussa

Permits from The Forestry Commission, Aros. (06803 346)

Loch Aros

Permits from Browns, Ironmongers, Tobermory. (0688 2020)

Loch Assapol

Permits from J. McKeand, Scoor House, Fionnphort. (06817 240). Argyll Arms Hotel, Bunessan. (06817 240) W.L. Rosier, Assapol House (06817 258)

Loch Ba

Enquire at Killichronan Estates. (06803 438)

Loch Frisa

Permits and boats from the Forestry Commission, Aros. (06803 346)

Loch Fuaron

Permits for part of the loch from Sandy Peddie, Rossal. (06814 210)

The Mishnish Lochs

Permits and boats from Browns, Ironmongers, Tobermory (0688 2020)

Loch Poit na h-I

Permits and boat from Pauline Anderson, Achaban Guest House, Fionnphort. (06817 205)

Loch Sguabain

Boat fishing only. Permits from Glenforsa Hotel, Aros (06803 377) Mull Travel, Craignure (06802 487) Tackle and Books,

Tobermory (0688 2336) McKeand, Scoor House, Fionnphort. (06817 297)

Loch Tor
Boats and permits from Tackle and Books, Tobermory. (0688 2336) or from Dick Fairbairns. Dervaig 275.

SEA ANGLING
Sea angling trips of various lengths in time and on various sizes of boats can be arranged by the following:
Dervaig
Richard Fairbairns. (06884 223)
Tobermory
Brian Swinbanks. (0688 2336)
Derek McAdam. (0688 2336)
Tackle and Books. (0688 2336)
Croig
Iain Morrison. (0688 4242)
Ulva Ferry
Brian Burgess. (0688 2165)

Eigg

It is doubtful if any Scottish island for its size has a more colourful history or unique natural features than tiny Eigg in the Western Hebrides. It is the second largest of the four small isles just south of Skye. It is only six miles long by four miles wide yet more seems to have happened on this little island than in many other larger areas of Britain.

In the spring of 617 the island's patron saint St Donnan landed with fifty monks to establish a mission. It was a short-lived attempt, as warriors from the North landed and killed all of them, apparently because they resented the monks Christianising the inhabitants. Although records of this are sketchy, there is a tradition that this bloodthirsty crew were led by a woman known as the Queen of the Pirates. She is supposed to have been a very large and domineering woman, indeed for centuries the island was often referred to as *Eilean nam Ban Mora*, Island of the Big Women. This is also the name of one of Eigg's lochs, and in an eyot in the middle of this loch there are traces of a dwelling.

A thousand years later there was another and more horrifying atrocity on the island, perhaps not unusual in the days of bloody clan feuds. In 1577 the MacLeods of Skye sailed for Eigg to avenge some real or supposed wrong done by the MacDonalds of Clan Ranald who were the owners and inhabitants of the island.

The islanders saw the armada of galleys from far off and this gave them time to conceal themselves — all 395 men, women and children — in a large cave called St Francis's Cave. Once everyone was inside they drew brushwood and vegetation over the small entrance and they were safe from discovery.

When the MacLeods came off their ships and searched for their prey, there was nobody to be found. The island seemed deserted. There was not even booty to be pillaged as the MacDonalds had taken all their smaller possessions to the cave with them. The invaders gave up their search and were actually sailing off for Skye when the inhabitants, weary of the confines of their cave, sent a scout to investigate the situation. He was spotted by someone on one of the galleys and the fleet turned round to land again on Eigg. The scout realised that he had been seen and, fearful for his own life, ran back to the cave. The ground was covered in recently-fallen snow and this left a clear set of footprints from the shore to the cave.

The MacLeods realised where their enemies were hiding and made straight for the cave. They called for the MacDonalds to come out and surrender. This brought no response because the MacDonalds knew they would be facing certain death.

Then the MacLeods prepared a deadly plan of extermination for their enemies. First they diverted a stream which was flowing over the cave's entrance, then they gathered heather and driftwood, piled it at the entrance to the cave and set it alight. They kept this fire blazing until all the MacDonalds in the cave were suffocated.

There is another tale of some violence from Eigg history going back to the early eighteenth century — this time with a happy ending. Donald MacQuarrie was a famous piper who lived in Grulin on the island and he married a girl called Catriona from the nearby island of Muck. Shortly after the marriage Catriona's two brothers heard that their sister was being ill-used by the piper. So they told her that if things got unbearable, all she had to do was light two fires on the foreshore opposite Muck.

One night the brothers saw the two fires blazing, came over to Eigg immediately, gave their brother-in-law a sound thrashing and took their sister home to Muck.

A few days later Donald MacQuarrie repented of his behaviour and was pining for Catriona to return. He took his bagpipes out to the cliffs facing the island of Muck and played a doleful lament that expressed his sorrow and repentance. Catriona sailed over to him, they were united and lived happily ever after.

Eigg was not spared the suffering of the other parts of the Highlands after the abortive 1745 rebellion in support of Bonnie Prince Charlie. A Captain Ferguson landed and captured a well-known Jacobite leader who had in his possession a list of names of supporters of the cause. These people were tricked into giving themselves up and imprisoned for a year, after which most of them ended their lives as slaves in the West Indies.

Neither was the island spared the ravages of the Highland Clearances. In 1853 a farmer from the Scottish Borders bought the island's comprehensive farm of Laig on the understanding that the land would be cleared of people in favour of sheep. That year fourteen families were evicted, most went to Nova Scotia.

It was not really until 1926 that the people of Eigg enjoyed reasonable security economically. That was when two wealthy brothers Viscount and Sir Steven Runciman rebuilt the Laird's house, revitalised the estate with capital, managed it progressively and reinvested all profits into it for the benefit of everyone on the island.

There is a curious and pleasant phenomenon in the north-west part of the island at a large stretch of bay called *Camus Sgiotaig* (The Bay of Musical Sand). This is a long beach of fine sand which creaks and hums under your feet like the sound of a harp, when you step on it in good weather. These are the Singing Sands of Eigg.

For all of its violent history, Eigg today is a lovely, verdant, peaceful little island, a jewel of beauty in the crown of the Hebrides.

Angling on Eigg

Finding freshwater places to fish on the island of Eigg is not at all easy. There are no streams to speak of and certainly none to provide any worthwhile game fishing. There are lochs but they are difficult to reach and surrounded by tricky bogland. But they *do* have some large trout, up to three pounds for those hardy fishers willing to make the trek.

Loch Nam Ban Mora is reckoned to be the best water — *if* you can reach it. The English translation of the name is 'Loch of the Big Women'. Perhaps they were undaunted in their trek!

Canna

If I didn't care if I ever fished again for a brown trout or a sea trout or a salmon but was content to catch sea fish not far from the shores of an idyllic Hebridean island and didn't mind camping, there is a lochless, riverless little island only a few miles from Mallaig called Canna. It is the most westerly of the Small Isles in the Inner Hebrides, the others being Rhum, Eigg and Muck.

Dr John Lorne Campbell, a world-famous Gaelic scholar and a legend in his own lifetime owned the island for many years. With his wife Margaret Fay Shaw who comes from Pennsylvania and who is also a famous scholar, he has spent years of dedication and care of the island and written authoritative books about it. In one of these he lists the fishes in the seas immediately around Canna which he has observed and identified:-

long-spined sea scorpion; grey gurnard; mackerel; Spanish mackerel; tunny; horse mackerel; John Dory; lump-sucker; grey mullets; ballan wrasse; striped, red and cuckoo wrasse; cod; haddock; saithe; whiting; pollack; ling; five-bearded rockling; greater sand eel; lesser sand eel; plaice; lemon sole; dab; flounder; sole; turbot; pipe-fish or needle-fish; herring; sprat; eel; conger; blue shark; basking shark; lesser spotted dogfish; skate; lamprey.

It has often struck me that if Dr Campbell's list is typical of the variety of sea fish waiting to be caught all over the Hebridean seas, it is little wonder that the various sea angling clubs have such an enthusiastic following in western Scotland.

Apart from its sea fish, Canna is unique and beautiful. It is nearly five miles long and a mile wide and all of it skirted by cliffs except the 1½-mile-long neighbouring island of Sanday (not a separate island when the tide is out) and the harbour. Up on Compass Hill the highly magnetised basalt upsets compass readings so much that the phenomenon is mentioned in the 'Sailing Directions' of the British Admiralty. As early as 1695 the traveller Martin Martin when he visited the Western Isles laid his compass on the stony ground near this high hill on the north end of the island and 'the needle went round and round with great swiftness, and instead of settling towards the north it settled due east'.

A family called Thom owned and resided in Canna from 1881 to 1938. Then the island was sold to Dr Lorne Campbell who was its owner until 1981 when he gave it and its neighbouring Sanday island to the National Trust for Scotland although he is still resident at Canna House. The island has been a bird sanctuary since 1938 and Dr Campbell its most dedicated observer and steward. With the gift of the island Dr Campbell also donated his large and extensive library of Gaelic literature and songs.

For those visiting sea anglers who feel they might like to cast a rod and line off Canna's shores, camping is really the only reliable means of accommodation. There are no roads on the island which operates as a single farm for sheep and cattle, although the National Trust for Scotland is experimenting with oyster farming. There is basic self-catering and bothy accommodation for short-term visitors.

How to get there? By ferry from Mallaig to Rhum and Canna is six miles from the northern tip of this island by boat to a surprisingly adequate harbour and pier.

OTHER ISLANDS IN THE AREA
Muck is the smallest of the Small Islands — sometimes called the Cocktail Islands — of Canna, Rhum and Eigg. The Gaelic meaning of its name is 'Island of pigs' really meaning the porpoises to be seen in shoals off the coast.

Skye

It would be surprising if the largest of all the Scottish islands did not have excellent fishing, particularly if that island has some of the grandest mountains and the most beautiful lochs in Britain — to say nothing of hundreds of miles of a coastline of rocks, shingle and glorious sands.

Skye has all of these things. But it all depends on what you might mean by 'excellent fishing'. Big salmon? No. The average size of fish on the Rivers Snizort and the Ose, for example, is around 7lb and the biggest Skye salmon caught in the last thirty years was no more than 15lb. Conversely, the Storr Lochs on the north-eastern wing of the island produce 800 trout in most seasons and the record here is a trout of 12lb. Around the coast some large sea fish have been taken — skate in excess of 100lb; conger larger than the Scottish boat record of 48lb and rays in the 12 to 15lb range.

So much for weight and numbers. But if those factors were the only ones to be filed under 'excellent' in the fishing archives, anglers might not wish to visit this history-laden, incredibly beautiful, romantic island only a few minutes by ferry from the Scottish mainland and of such irresistible attraction that thousands of tourists return year after year just to be within sight of the Cuillins and the majesty of the other mountains. And this does not even take into account the magnificent malt whisky distilled there.

Skye is an island for anglers who consider the fishing first and the fish second. Environment is everything and the main reason that hordes of rock climbers and 'mountain people' come every year to face the great challenges of the Skye peaks. It is also the island of the romantics with its connections with Bonnie Prince Charlie and Flora MacDonald and that last great adventure of the Scottish Highland clans in 1745.

The salmon angler will find nothing of the attractions of the Tay or the Spey or other famous mainland rivers. Most of the rivers on Skye are spate rivers and without rain they can be reduced to mere streams. The rise and fall, however, is sudden and extreme, mainly because most of them run through impervious rocks and do not have the 'sponge' advantage of peat. For the same reason, the rivers which drain off the central part of the island are usually very clear and free of peat-staining even when in flood. These rivers include the Broadford, Camasunory, Coruisk, Drynoch, Brittle, Kilmarie and Sligachan. Other rivers which *do* become peaty coloured in spate are the Snizort, Varagill and Ose.

Because of the rapid rise and fall of these spate rivers, salmon often become trapped in the pools and this encourages poachers who find it easy to get their prey, although their haul for the most part consists of grilse and small salmon. Poaching is an endemic malady in Skye and guarding the rivers in these wilderness areas an almost impossible task.

Most of the salmon fishing is in private hands although the main river Snizort is available to guests of the local hotel as are the Ose and the Sligachan. Indeed nearly every hotel on the island has access to some river salmon fishing and sea trout and brown trout fishing.

Depending on the water level of the various rivers, the salmon start ascending from the end of July and sea trout start to appear in the tidal pools in June.

A look at the map of Skye shows why it got the Gaelic name of 'The Flying Island' with its projection-like wings. It is about fifty miles from north-west to south-east and forty-five miles in width at its extremities. Skye has been for so long romantically described, set to music, recited in poetry, its history related so often that even those who have never been there feel they know it. 'Over the sea to Skye' and the 'Skye boatman's song' have brought a misty eye to many exiled Scots all over the world.

Going round the island, a visitor with a twitchy wrist and a fishing rod will have little difficulty finding fishing hotels with access to salmon fishing. Whether there is water or not in the river, of course, is another matter. Struan, Bracadale, Duntulm, Dunvegan, Sleat, Skeabost, Sligachan, Staffin and Uig are all good centres for hotel waters. However, Portree is really the main town from which to obtain permits and advice. Moreover, what are probably Skye's best trout lochs are only a few miles north of the town — the Storr Lochs. These inter-linked lochs are well managed by Portree Angling Association and permits for either bank or boat fishing obtained from the Association's premises in the Masonic Buildings in Portree. They have ten well-maintained boats.

The last time I fished the Storr Lochs was most enjoyable. I had an offer from a fish every fourth or fifth cast and although my basket of four fish was not spectacular — all about ¾lb — I did lose another couple that were well above that weight. I was told that 2lb and 3lb fish are taken frequently.

Other waters managed by the Portree Angling Association are the fourteen hill lochs in the north part of the island. Most other trout lochs are managed by the hotels in the areas shown above.

Nearly two-thirds of the place-names in Skye are of old Norse origin. For example, the name Cuillin is a plural noun from Kjöllen meaning 'keel-shaped ridges'. Groups of mountains of the same name are found in Iceland and Sweden.

Sir Walter Scott's novel *The Lord of the Isles* provided inspiration a hundred years ago for artists and writers, particularly around Loch Coruisk when there were probably more landscape painters to be seen than either climbers or anglers. Nearly every British painter of note felt he had to paint Coruisk — Turner, Horatio MacCulloch, MacWhirter, Alfred Williams, George Fennel Robson and many others. Those plus the scores of writers described the 1½ miles length of the loch with all its beautiful characteristics except, it seems, the fishing.

One type of angling not at all dependent on rainfall or other weather factors on the island is sea fishing. The waters around Skye are teeming with skate, tope, dogfish, conger, rays, wrasse, haddock and, of course, cod. The favourite marks for fishing from boat or shore are described very well in the booklet *Sea Angling Guide to Skye* written by Gus MacDonald and on sale at the tourist offices or in the local shops. According to the author, the best fishing on the island is from Moonen Bay near Dunvegan.

Boats for hire or charter are in abundance around the coast of Skye and there are adequate bait locations for digging and gathering lugworm, rockworm, ragworm, crabs, limpets, cockles and mussels. The main centre for sea angling activities and the hire of boats is Portree although there are good facilities at Dunvegan, Glendale, Broadford and Uig.

There were two sea angling clubs on Skye for many years but recently the North West Skye club merged with the Isle of Skye club and the twenty-odd members are enthusiastic and willing to host any visitors who might like to join them on an outing. George Smith, the secretary, is in Portree.

OTHER ISLANDS IN THE AREA

Eilean Ban. Some writers have been known to fall in love at first sight with an island. And this tiny island — only twelve acres — is one of these. It lies in the narrow sound at the Kyle of Lochalsh between Skye and the mainland. John Buchan became so entranced with its incredible beauty and its dazzling white sands that he used it in his book *A Prince of the Captivity.* Then years later Gavin Maxwell bought the island to convert it into a zoo containing west Highland animals and birds. When he died the project ended although his partner Sir John Lister-Kaye wrote a book about the island and the project.

Scalpay. There are two islands of this name in the Hebrides. The first is half a mile from Skye by Loch Ainort and has a tiny population and a poor economy.

Soay. The Norse name means 'Isle of sheep' and this island is not to be confused with Solay in St Kilda or Soay in Orkney. This one is on the western seaboard of Skye and has a population of fifty. Lobster fishing is the main occupation but recently an artists' colony has been developed on the island.

It was on this island that Gavin Maxwell lived and based his ill-fated shark-hunting enterprise which he described in his book *Harpoon at a Venture.*

Where to get Permission to Fish

FRESHWATER FISHING

Bracadale

Shops in Struan will give information on salmon, sea trout and brown trout fishing available in the area.

Broadford

Fishing on the Broadford River is free to hotel guests at the Broadford Hotel.

Duntulm

The local hotel has salmon, sea trout and brown trout fishing on the Kilmartin and the Kilmaling Rivers.

Dunvegan

The Dunvegan Hotel has fishing rights on numerous rivers and lochs in the area and issues daily and weekly permits. Boats can be arranged through Captain Henderson, 17 Skinidin, Glendale. (Glendale 268)

Sleat

Isle of Ornsay Hotel has trout and sea trout fishing on many rivers and lochs in the area and issues daily and weekly tickets. Free to hotel guests. Also Kinloch Lodge Hotel.

Portree

Portree Angling Association issues daily and weekly tickets for their excellent lochs about two miles from the town. Contact the Association at Masonic Buildings, Portree.

Struan

Ulinish Lodge Hotel has fishing on Loch Connan and other lochs. (Struan 214)

Staffin
Permits to fish lochs in the area can be obtained from the Gamekeeper's Cottage, Staffin.

Skeabost
Skeabost House Hotel has eight miles of salmon and sea trout fishing on the River Snizort.

Sligachan
Sligachan Hotel has salmon and sea trout fishing on two miles of the Sligachan River, also brown trout fishing on lochs. Free to hotel guests.

Uig
Uig Hotel can arrange fishing on north bank of River Hinnisdale. Also fishing on Storr Lochs.

SEA ANGLING
Many of these hotels can hire boats or otherwise arrange for sea angling trips:
Duntulm Hotel
Isle of Ornsay Hotel, Sleat
Skeabost House Hotel.

The Two Borerays

There are two islands off Scotland called Boreray and they are very different although within about fifty miles of each other.

One of them is not much more than a great rock far out in the Atlantic off the island of St Kilda. It lies forty-one miles North-north-west of Griminish Point in North Uist. This Boreray is a huge, awesome rock with cliffs a thousand feet high and steely, sea-polished surfaces that would make either landing or climbing almost impossible. The island is shaped like a dog-tooth, one side falling into the sea like an immense wall and the other side tilted.

In spite of the terrible risks involved, the men of St Kilda used to hunt the sea-birds on these formidable cliffs. There is a story that 120 years ago they caught a great auk which was the last one ever seen in Britain. They thought it was a witch in disguise and beat it to death.

This Boreray has two satellites, Stac Lee and Stac an Armin and these three constitute the largest gannetry in the world. A count in 1959 put the number at approximately 20,000 nesting pairs and this is reckoned to be about a seventh of the world's gannets. Where there are sea-birds there are fish and the obvious conclusion is that the seas around this island must produce a rich harvest.

The *other* Boreray is a gentler island altogether. It lies about a mile off the north-east tip of North Uist and is 4½ miles in circumference. Its highest point is 176 feet and the northern part of the island only 50 feet above sea level. It is a fertile island and back in 1845 thirty families lived there in relative comfort. But in 1921 the population was down to sixty-three then later it was down to three men and three women. Today there is only one family.

Martin Martin the early and famous explorer and writer of the Highlands and Islands tells how a Dutchman, Captain Peters, sheltered his ship in the lee of Boreray in the late seventeenth century. One of his crew went ashore and returned with a tale of how he encountered ten women 'employed in a strange manner'. What he witnessed was one of the earliest descriptions of making what we now know as Harris Tweed.

In his same journal, Martin also wrote: 'In the middle of this island, there's a Fresh Water Lake, well stock'd with very big Eels, some of them as long as Cod, or Ling-fish; there is a passage under the Stony Ground, which is between the Sea and the Lake, through which it's suppos'd the Eels came in with the Spring Tides; one of the Inhabitants called Mack-Vanish, i.e. Monks-son, had the curiosity to creep naked through this Passage.'

Today what is left of Boreray village lies in a bay on the western side of the island and a small stream runs through it. There is a large loch — doubtless the one referred to by Martin — called Loch Mor which becomes brackish when the sea breaks over the narrow strip separating it from the ocean.

Coll

That indispensable book *Where to fish* edited by D.A. Orton published annually by Thomas Harmsworth Publishing Co says that all the loch fishing on Coll is privately-owned. Since there are over thirty lochs large and small on the island, I would find it hard to believe that a request to one of the three owners — C.K.M. Stewart, J. de Vries and Mrs Erskine — would not bring permission to fish a few of them. It would also be surprising if the one and only hotel at Arinagour could not oblige.

There is no record of huge fish being caught on Coll, certainly no salmon probably because there are no streams (the highest point on the island is only 330 feet). But earlier sportsmen who have visited the island with a fishing rod have described their experience among those lochs and lochans as superb. Their casting for the half-pound — and occasionally the pound — trout has been an idyll. The tranquillity and magnetising beauty of Coll has impressed them more than any challenge of the fish.

There are two meanings in the Gaelic language for the name of the island. One of them is *Colla Creagach* — rocky Coll. The other applies more particularly to the verdant interior of the island or to the magnificent Atlantic-washed beaches of the north-west coast — *Colla Boidheach* — beautiful Coll.

The sea fishing around Coll is very good. Those Atlantic rollers which pound the north-west beaches stir up a bounty of feeding for the teeming fish in these waters and sea anglers can reap the benefit.

King Robert the Bruce gave Coll to Angus Og of the Isles in the 13th century and it was then held by the McLeans who built Breachacha Castle. This is now a ruin.

In 1773 Dr Johnson and his friend Boswell were sailing from Skye to Mull when their boat was blown ashore in a storm and they were kept on Coll by the weather for ten days. He praised the place and the sturdy, self-supporting character of the people. The young laird entertained his guests royally and Dr Johnson met a young man from the island who walked each year across Scotland to Aberdeen to attend the brief university session then walked back every winter to earn a little money teaching the island children as there was no other teacher.

There used to be two thousand inhabitants on Coll; now there are 150, half of them living in or near Arinagour village where a new pier was built in 1969 to accommodate the car ferry from Oban. There is also an airport to serve the regular flights from Glasgow and elsewhere.

Coll is an island for those who love the enchantment of the Hebrides, who want peace and unhurried days in a beautiful environment.

Where to get permission to fish
FRESHWATER FISHING AND SEA ANGLING
There is no stream or river fishing on the island but numerous lochs. Details of the fishing available on these and the sea fishing around the island can be obtained by booking into the Isle of Coll Hotel, Arinagour, Isle of Coll. (Coll 334)

Tiree

Although it does have four hills each over 100 feet, this island of Tiree, twelve miles long and six miles at its widest has a popular name in the Gaelic language *Tir fo Thuinn* 'The land below the waves'. It is very flat, very beautiful, sunny most of the time and very breezy as the Atlantic winds blow unhindered across its shallow land. It is also very fertile and it has another Gaelic nickname 'The granary of the islands'. Even today the cattle raised on Tiree meadows just up from the shores are prized everywhere and fetch the best possible prices when sold.

The main reason for this abundance of growth and pasture and flowers on the machairs, those verdant stretches just up from the beaches, is that the crushed shells provide calcareous soil which is easily ploughed and promotes excellent growth. It drains freely, so much of the island's economy has always been based on agriculture.

You get to Tiree from Oban by boat and the journey takes four hours. Of course, you can fly if you are in a hurry although why on earth anyone would wish to be in a hurry in such a lovely place as the Inner Hebrides of Scotland is beyond comprehension. Tiree has the lowest rainfall and the sunniest climate in Scotland.

In a way it was Tiree's excellent fertility and potential for crops and cattle-raising which caused a minor civil war in 1885. Many people were cleared off the island so that large farms could be created and tenants installed. Those who remained revolted and the British naval vessel HMS *Ajax* was sent to quell the disturbance with thirty soldiers. The ringleaders were arrested and imprisoned and the soldiers stayed on to help to gather the harvest. The following year the Crofters' Act was passed and the big farms were broken up.

For all its agricultural prosperity, Tiree is a remote place and the young people tend to leave the island for jobs and careers elsewhere. Two hundred years ago the population was three times what is today.

It is the machair lochs that are of interest to the angler. These are the low-lying waters on raised beaches where the underlying soil is rich and promotes plentiful life and feeding for trout. These fish come out at least a pound in weight and some are as big as four pounds. Loch a' Phuil behind Balephuil Bay is one of these and another is Loch Bharrapol. Indeed these are the only two lochs worth the attention of the serious trout angler. The problem about them for a visitor is that both are strictly private and controlled by a syndicate. However, it is possible to be considered for a permit by application to the Factor at Argyll Estate Office, Heylipol, Scarinish on the island.

Yes, there are other lochs containing trout on the island and permission to fish these is usually easier to obtain. But the fishing is not in the same class as the two lochs mentioned above.

Where to get Permission to Fish
Trout fishing on the two lochs on Tiree is not easily available but request should be made to The Factor, Argyll Estate Office, Heylipol, Scarinish, Isle of Tiree, Argyll. (Scarinish 516)

Raasay
It is difficult to find an island in the Western Highlands of Scotland which is not distinguished one way or another by its beauty, its colourful history, the quality of its fishing or simply the romantic dream-like magnetism so common in the Hebrides.

The island of Raasay comes very near to being the opposite of all these things. It is an island just off the Skye mainland to which a small ferry plies every day across the short Sound of Raasay. It measures 13 miles by 3½ miles and a visitor — even someone with a fishing rod — might find it hard going to have their interest sustained.

Somehow it all seemed so very different back in 1773 when Dr Johnson and James Boswell visited the place during their famous tour of the Highlands. They were entertained royally at Raasay House. Johnson wrote about the adventure:

'The boat was under the direction of Mr Malcolm MacLeod, a gentleman of Raasay. The water was calm, and the rowers were vigorous, so that our passage was quick and pleasant. When we came near the island, we saw the laird's house, a neat, modern fabrick, and found Mr MacLeod, the proprietor of the island, with many gentlemen, expecting us on the beach. We had, as at all other places, some difficulty in landing. The crags were irregularly broken, and a false step could have been very mischievous.'

From all accounts, even if Raasay was a rather dull place in Dr Johnson's time, he and Boswell certainly made up for any boredom. The family at Raasay consisted of the laird, his lady, three sons and ten daughters. The party ate a sumptuous meal, wined very well, then the Doctor and Boswell danced the night through with the daughters.

The population of Raasay is 160 and this is about a third of what it was a hundred years ago. The reason for the exodus, of course, was the same as that on most of the other Hebridean islands during the Clearances when the people were removed to make way for sheep.

The earliest known record of the island is an account of King Haakon's expedition to Scotland in 1262 when the Norwegian war galleys were on their way to Largs, the battlefield where the following year the Norsemen were defeated. Since then the story of Raasay is one of clan feuds and violence and takeovers. There is ample record of the MacLeods' scheming, raiding and robberies. There was a disastrous potato famine in 1846 when the then laird, John MacLeod, sold his island estates and sailed for Tasmania. The new owner was Mr Rainy of Edinburgh who followed the ruthless route of many other landowners at the time and forcibly evicted the tenants. A hundred and twenty-nine families were shipped to Australia. Those who refused to go were moved to the neighbouring island of Rona where starvation and typhoid took their toll.

So far as sports fishing is concerned, there seems to be no waters particularly outstanding either for the quality or quantity. Any guidebook you consult will simply tell you that the fishing is free and that an angler may fish any of the lochs or streams.

Lest I condemn Raasay for anglers as having no importance at all, the island does have a place in fishing history. There is a salmon fishing station at Brochel and there is record there of a fish caught in the nets a few years back called the Angler Fish. This grotesque fish is very rarely caught off the British coasts. It is a fish which attracts its prey by waving a filament similar to a small fishing rod in front of its large mouth. There is a form of hook on the end — hence the name.

This particular fish was quite small but there is also record of a Mr Dunn of Cornwall bringing ashore such a fish of 20 feet in length and 18 inches in width.

I feel sure that the island of Raasay will distinguish itself for game fishers in some other acceptable way within the next few years. It certainly deserves it.

Where to get Permission to Fish
FRESHWATER FISHING
Free trout fishing in lochs and streams. Spare waders and tackle should be taken.

Rhum

Among the hundreds of islands around Scotland there are many which have been described as 'The island that likes to be visited'. Indeed J.M. Barrie wrote a very popular play *Mary Rose* with just this theme about a Hebridean island.

The little islands in the Sea of the Hebrides between the Scottish mainland and Skye are Rhum, Eigg, Muck, Canna and Sanday. The largest, and certainly the most mountainous, of these is Rhum which is diamond-shaped and measures only eight miles by eight miles. There are no roads, no easy shores or bays for landing boats; dogs or cats are forbidden; visits have to be carefully arranged beforehand and trips on the island are carefully restricted to certain routes at certain times. Of course, there are good reasons for these strictures. Today Rhum is a 'living laboratory' for the study of deer, birds, plants and other wildlife.

It is an island with a sad history. It only became part of the Scottish Kingdom in 1266. Before that it belonged to the Norsemen and before that to Irish settlers.

From the time the island became Scottish it was owned, sold, stolen, resold and resettled many times by a succession of clan chiefs. Later when cattle prices fell after the Napoleonic Wars and people were being replaced by sheep, Rhum did not escape the notorious Clearances organised by lairds and their factors. When 300 inhabitants sailed in the *Dove of Harmony* and *Highland Lad* to Canada, only fifty people remained on the island. Two years later, half-starved, they too left for Nova Scotia.

It was the second Marquis of Salisbury who bought the island in 1845, stocked the hills with deer and gave the whole island to his son who initiated another Clearance to Canada two years later. One family leaving could trace its history back to 1386.

Today Rhum holds a peculiar fascination for people who visit it, in spite of its forbidding history and its somewhat restrictive present. Indeed few visit the island once only — in spite of the midges and other insects in summer! The late Gavin Maxwell gave this view of the island in his book *Harpoon at a Venture*:

'Rhum is a strange place, eery and haunted if ever a Hebridean island was. It is all mountain — hills as dark and savage as the Cuillins themselves and falling for the most part steeply to the sea. The hills even carry the name, the Cuillins of Rhum, but they seem to have a different soul, something older and more brooding. The names are mainly Norse, given them long ago by the raiding longships. If there is a place where I could believe every Gaelic folk-tale and superstition it is in their shadow. I know a man who found himself in a high corner of Askival with a dead stag after dusk. His coat was clutched and he felt himself being dragged uphill, while from right below his feet, a voice seemed in an extremity of fear.'

From 1845 Rhum was a private sporting estate and access to it was consistently discouraged. The whole island was as private as if it was a person's exclusive garden — which, in a way it was. This was particularly true during the ownership of the Bullough family which began in 1887 and lasted right up to 1957 when the Nature Conservancy Council bought it for £23,000 from Monica, Lady Bullough, widow of Sir George Bullough who was knighted in 1910 and made a baronet six years later and who died in 1939. The sale included Kinloch Castle which had been built at a cost of a quarter of a million pounds by Sir George.

In a way, however disagreeable it may have been to 'outsiders', the exclusive and conservative restrictions which the Bulloughs exercised were a benefit. Although it was recognised during the family's residence as 'The Forbidden Island', the discouragement of visitors did preserve the deer and the bird and plant life. It was this factor which doubtless encouraged the Nature Conservancy Council to purchase the island. Its 26,400 acres (100 are woodland) became an area of exceptional interest for research. It is now the main centre in Britain for the study of Red Deer (there are about 1500 today). Since the takeover as a 'living laboratory', 2158 species of insects have been recorded and 51 species of spiders alone. There is also a special breed of Rhum ponies which grow to a height of only fourteen hands; they say they are the descendants of survivors from a galleon of the Spanish Armada wrecked on the coast in 1588.

Since the Council took over the island, 'forbidden island' or not, more than 8000 people set foot on it in the first six years, half of these day visitors from Mallaig or Skye. The only practical anchorage or landing area is at Loch Sceresort on the east side.

John Bullough was a wealthy textile machinery manufacturer who came from Accrington. The building of Kinloch Castle was his lifetime's ambition. Today, although it is remarkably well maintained, it is something of a white elephant. Some critics have described the vast interior as a sort of 'Xanadu', heavy and tasteless, over-furnished with somewhat vulgar pieces. The baths have to be seen to be believed — they are huge and have taps for almost every conceivable purpose.

Sixteen guests can now be accommodated in the Castle with a tariff of around £50 per person for dinner, bed and breakfast. At the back of the castle, in what were originally the servants' quarters, there is a hostel run on a self-catering basis the charge for which is only a few pounds per day.

For all the restrictions there is still a lot to do on Rhum. But the wild beauty of the place with its unique wildlife makes a trip well worthwhile for people who like hiking and can ignore the midges! Waterproof clothing with good sturdy footwear are essential.

The Forbidden Island has opened its gates at last.

Fishing on Rhum

Yes, there *is* fishing to be had on the 'Forbidden Island' of Rhum. Here is what the Chief Warden of the Rhum National Nature Reserve has to say about it:

'Most, if not all, who fish on Rhum will be staying for a while in a range of accommodation from camping, bothies, hostel or Kinloch Castle Hotel. The fishing available is on hill lochs, the actual ones available at the time, especially in the spring, being determined by checking for Schedule 1 bird breeding/nesting activity. This still leaves a number available for brown trout fishing.

'A daily permit has to be obtained from the Reserve Office and we ask for returns to be submitted to enable us to keep records. Spinning and fly are generally the techniques used. There is no river fishing currently available but we have no objection to fishing off the rocks above the coast except in the north of the island at Kilmory which is an area generally closed for red deer research.'

Where to Get Permission to Fish

FRESHWATER FISHING AND SEA ANGLING

Brown trout fishing on a number of hill lochs may be arranged by application to the Chief Warden of the Nature Conservancy Council at White House, Isle of Rhum. Tel: (0687 2026)

The Council have no objection to sea fishing off the rocks around the coast except in the north of the island at Kilmory.

Accommodation is limited to Kinloch Castle and the hostel at the rear of the castle.

Eriskay

There are some islands around Scotland, as indeed there are elsewhere in the world, which seem to have a destiny for dullness. Nothing happens and they are famous for nothing. And very little of importance has happened to them through history. As a rule they are lonely places, unsung, unheralded, most uninhabited and without even a good, old-fashioned legend to lift them from obscurity — not even an untrue one.

Conversely, there are others which for size seem to have been endowed with all the drama and tradition and interest that any island could wish for. Eriskay is one of these.

It is an island off the southern shores of South Uist and north of Barra in the Western Hebrides, a small, beautiful, quiet place only 3½ miles by 1½ miles wide. Even those who have never visited it are moved to hear the famous Eriskay Love Lilt being sung.

The people speak Gaelic and are in the main Roman Catholic. They are warm, kindly and hardworking.

Although it was Compton MacKenzie who brought out all the romance and humour of Eriskay in his book *Whisky Galore*, the island has always seemed to be waiting for stories to be told about it. MacKenzie's book is based on the story of the S.S. *Politician* which ran aground having mistaken the Sound of Eriskay for the Sound of Barra on her way to America carrying 24,000 cases of whisky.

There is a certain fitness about this story because Eriskay has had quite a history of using the proceeds of wrecks. In 1903 Father Allan MacDonald persuaded the fishermen to contribute one day's catch towards building the local Catholic church St Michael's at Rhuban. He designed the church himself and the church bell comes from the German battleship *Der Lingir* sunk in Scapa Flow. And the altar was created later out of a local wreck by Father Callum MacNeil. Other pieces in the building of the chapel have been used from washed-up wreckage.

Eriskay was the first piece of land on which Prince Charles Edward Stuart — claimant to the British crown — set his foot. He anchored his ship off the Prince's Strand on 23 July 1745 and came ashore disguised as a young priest. The people of Eriskay did not offer him much hospitality and he had to catch flounders off the sandy beach for his supper and he slept that night in a broken-down hut. By the time he left, however, the Prince had bequeathed Eriskay two famous things — the recipe for the famous Drambuie liqueur and the beautiful, pink sea bindweed *Calystegia Solkdanella* known as the Prince's flower. They say it will not grow anywhere else in Scotland.

Apart from the island's tranquillity and scenic beauty, it is famous for its breed of Eriskay ponies, small docile and hardy animals. The breed is very old and is reckoned to be the nearest type to the native one that was in Scotland before man.

Although crofting is the main occupation on the island the Eriskay men are very skilled and successful fishermen. The seas around the island and in the Sound of Eriskay are rich in fish life. There should be no difficulty for a visitor to find an obliging fisherman to take him on an outing with rod and line.

Barra

On the islands around Scotland there are many ways for a visiting angler to get permission to fish, to find out where to go, how to get to know the waters, to find out what kind of tackle to use and what flies to choose. On some islands there is a helpful angling association and a visit to the local secretary usually brings the best of advice and permission to fish their waters at moderate cost. On some islands the local tourist office is quite knowledgeable and will sell permits and often a fishing map to the visitor. For those anglers not averse to paying a bit more for a fishing beat, there are private estates which own their own waters and it is usually wise to book such fishing well in advance; a least of a week or more is not unusual on such waters.

Fishing tackle shops in the main towns on the islands are the best places to go initially. Tacklists are very well informed about the angling opportunities and most sell permits for local waters. And for sea anglers the most obvious place to go is to the harbour where just about everybody knows who hires or charters boats and what the charges may be.

There is, however, one other very important source of information and service for the visiting angler — the local hotels on the island. Most hotels in Scotland cater for guests with all kinds of pursuits and interests and it would be difficult to find a hotel on any of the islands which did not serve the angler with all his needs if he stays in the hotel.

One island where this is particularly true is Barra which lies at the southern tip of the Outer Hebrides chain of islands. Although there is no salmon fishing available, there is some good trout fishing in the lochs and all three hotels on the island issue permits as well as arranging sea fishing trips. Indeed it is the sea fishing which is becoming more and more popular on Barra and the fishing grounds off the island's coasts are rich in all type of fish. The coastline varies from sheltered inlets and the fine harbours of Castlebay and Northbay to high cliffs and wide sandy bays fringed by huge sand dunes. This variety of sea-beds provides great variety of fishing from flat fish to cod.

Castlebay is the main town on the island and is the harbour for the car ferry service to Oban and South Uist. It overlooks Scotland's oldest castle Kiessimul which was built about 1060 and is the stronghold of the MacNeils who were given Barra by King Robert the Bruce. For a couple of centuries the MacNeil clan was notorious for piracy raids on the north of Ireland before settling down to more peaceful occupations on Barra. In 1838 the clan chief sold the island, then in 1937 a descendent bought back the castle and restored it to its former glory. Barra is sometimes called the Garden of the Hebrides simply because the machair (meadowlands) on this small island (8 miles by 4½ miles) are carpeted with wild flowers and their bloom is beautiful in springtime. The beach along the edge of the Traigh Mhor is a wide and shallow bay of shell (mainly cockleshells) and sand. On the rim of the sea-meadow is the house built by Sir Compton MacKenzie as his Hebridean home. It is now the headquarters for a company which makes rough cast from the cockleshells. This beach is probably the only airstrip in the world where 'plane arrivals are conditioned by the twice-a-day tides because this is where the 'planes from Glasgow and Benbecula land on the wet sand.

OTHER ISLANDS IN THE AREA

Fuday in the Sound of Barra was used as a burial ground by the Norsemen and signs of graves can still be seen in the sands on this uninhabited island.

Fiaray is supposed to have a fairy woman who can be seen by passing fishing boats. The island is situated north of Barra.

Mingulay is the second-last island in the Outer Hebrides 'chain' which ends south of Barra. It is 2½ miles long by 1½ miles across and is uninhabited. In 1881 it used to have eight farms and a population of 150 people.

Sandray is half a mile south of Vatersay and has been deserted since 1934. It has a loch and two streams which were at one time quite famed for game fishing.

Vatersay is half a mile off the southern shore of Barra. It has a population of about eighty who are Gaelic-speaking and Roman Catholic. However small, the island has had its own share of drama. In 1908 the inhabitants of the nearby island of Mingulay were starving and they moved to Vatersay where they built themselves wooden shacks and 'squatted'. They were charged by the absentee landlord of land-grabbing and all were sentenced to a term of imprisonment. When they came out they were — and still are — hailed as local heroes for standing up to the landlord who never even visited the island.

Although they were sentenced to six months in the Calton Jail in Edinburgh, so great was the public outcry in their favour that they were released in six weeks and allowed to return to Vatersay.

Earlier — in 1853 — a ship the *Annie Jane* carrying emigrants from Liverpool to Quebec foundered and sank just off Vatersay. Three quarters of all those aboard drowned.

Vatersay must now be considered an island in the *past* tense because a causeway has been built linking it with the mainland of Barra.

Other islands in the area of Barra are Gighay, Hellisay and Muldoanich.

Where to Get Permission to Fish
FRESHWATER FISHING AND SEA ANGLING

Facilities for both sports (trout fishing on lochs, there are no rivers) can be arranged for guests in any of the three hotels on the island:

Castlebay Hotel, Castlebay, Isle of Barra, Outer Hebrides. PA80 5XD (Castlebay 223)

Isle of Barra Hotel, Tangasdale Beach, Isle of Barra, Outer Hebrides PA80 5XW (08714 383)

Clachan Beag Hotel, Castlebay. (0870 2024)

Islands in the West

The rugged and indented western coastline of Scotland has scattered about it islands large and small.

Kerrera stands as a shelter to the harbour of Oban and lies between Mull and the mainland. It was here the Viking armada rested before sailing south to the Battle of Largs where they were defeated.

Lismore means 'great enclosure'. Lismore is a long, narrow island with its 'stern' in Loch Linnhe and its 'bow' pointing into the Firth of Lorne. It is quite treeless but very fertile, sheltered by the mountains of Appin and Morvern. It was once the site of a Christian settlement almost as important as Iona.

Lunga is to the east of Mull and in the Firth of Lorne among a scattering of small islands. There used to be a slate-cutting industry on the island and some of these slates were sent to roof the abbey in Iona.

Seil Island is hardly an island at all because it is linked to the mainland near Oban and access to it is by a humpback bridge designed by Thomas Telford in 1792. It is called 'The bridge over the Atlantic'.

Islands in the North-West of Scotland

Up in the north-west of Scotland there are some islands worth the attention of a visitor who might like to know their background.

Handa has been a bird sanctuary since 1962 when the Royal Society for the Protection of Birds took over the island's 766 acres and refurbished the only available building as a base. It is near Scourie in north-west Sutherland and its cliffs are 400 feet high. It was once populated by seven families and governed by an island queen who was always the oldest widow.

The Summer Isles is an archipelago of a dozen islands of different shapes and sizes dotted at the entrance to Loch Broom and they are so-called because in summer the crofters from Achiltibuie grazed their sheep on them. The main islands are Tanera Mor, Tanera Beg, Priest Island, Horse Island, Isle Ristol and Isle Martin.

The islets and creeks of Loch Broom provide good shelter for small boats thus making the whole area excellent for sea angling.

Priest Island has excellent trout fishing on its eight lochans.

Carn Islands are west of the mainland near the Summer Isles in Loch Broom and there are five of them. When the herring boom was in full swing, people lived on this island but now it is virtually uninhabited.

Isle of Ewe lies in the middle of Loch Ewe. It is privately-owned and somewhat undistinguished although it was at the hub of an important naval base during World War 2.

Other islands in the north-west are Gruinard, Oldany and Rabbit Island.

3. The Outer Hebrides

Benbecula

*I*t used to be an island. That was when the only way you could get to Benbecula from North Uist or South Uist was on foot or by horse and cart across the dangerous shifting sands. Then in 1943 they built a causeway over the South Ford and in 1950 the link to North Uist was opened by the Queen Mother. So now there is a roadway right down through the Uists and Benbecula is no longer an island — at least geographically. The people there still see themselves as something 'different'.

Different or not, it is in this small area only seven miles across that an example of inter-religious tolerance is practised for the world to see. Half the inhabitants share the Roman Catholic faith of South Uist and half belong to the Church of Scotland.

What is puzzling is the name. Benbecula in Gaelic means 'Mountain of the fords'. There is only one hill on the island, Rueval, and it was here in a cave that Prince Charles Edward Stuart hid waiting for Flora MacDonald while on his flight from Scotland after the abortive 1745 rebellion of the Highlanders. The rest of the island is quite flat and it is a task for the visitor to know which is land and which is water. It would be difficult to throw a stone and guarantee hitting dry land.

For a visiting angler, the place is an Elysium. There are no rivers but the lochs, the number of which nobody has tried to count, simply festoon the whole landscape. All of them have trout — some have sea trout — and permission to fish is usually very easy to get. A few of the lochs are preserved by local riparian owners, for instance Loch Olavat (it is in two parts) which is in the centre of the island, Loch Heouravay and Loch Langavat which also have occasional sea trout. Almost anyone in Benbecula knows who owns or manages what loch. South Uist Angling Association has most of them and the Creagurry Hotel issues permits to its own guests.

Much of the island consists of sandy machair, strips of green grassland, although much of the east side is taken up with bogland. For non-angling visitors, there is the ruined Borve Castle in a field close to the main road. This is a fourteenth century building and was the stronghold of the Clan Ranald. A couple of miles further north is the fourteenth century Nunton Chapel destroyed to a large extent after the reformation. Some of the lochs on Benbecula have traces of civilisations dating from the first and second centuries.

An angler on Benbecula is really spoiled for choice. He is surrounded by lochs and voes and inlets and sea-pools all of which have fish ranging from half-pound brown trout to three or four pounds sea trout. It is hard to know where to cast a fly but the visiting enthusiast should head straight for Loch Olavat or Loch Ba Alasdair. Permission to fish these can be obtained from the area office of the Ministry of Agriculture and Fisheries in Balivanich.

OTHER ISLANDS IN THE AREA

Wiay is an uninhabited little island off the south-east corner of Benbecula and was in the news a few years ago when a large brown bear made its home there after escaping from a filming session in Benbecula. It swam the short distance between the two islands. Twenty-two days later it was recaptured in North Uist.

Other islands in the vicinity of Benbecula are Grimsay and Ronay.

Where to Get Permission to Fish
FRESHWATER FISHING

Creagorry Hotel has free fishing for guests on several lochs giving good sea trout and brown trout fishing, also three good sea pools (Benbecula 2024). South Uist Angling Club has rights on 15 lochs, four with boats.

Four lochs south of Balivanich may be fished with permission from Department of Agriculture and Fisheries, Area Office, Balivanich. (Benbecula 234)

The Uists

We call them islands but some have barely made it. In the Outer Hebrides where the Atlantic gales have been pounding these scrags of western Scotland for millions of years, it is sometimes hard to know what is an island and what is not.

Lewis is attached to Harris in the southern part by a geographical hairsbreadth. Until 1961 there was an island called North Uist and one called South Uist. In that year it all changed when the Queen Mother officially opened the causeway linking the two parts and took another island Benbecula in its stride. Now we tend to call them the Uists because it is quite possible to drive right down the 'spine' of them starting from Lochmaddy in the north, going through Benbecula into South Uist and terminating at the port of Lochboisdale at the bottom.

The Uists and Benbecula are an area virtually designed by nature for anglers. The whole countryside on either side of that causeway backbone from north to south is festooned with lochs, lochs, lochs. Indeed it is possible in places to stop the car, get out, set up a fishing rod, make a few casts to the right on to a loch, then make a few casts to the left on to another loch. And it is highly probable you would get a fish from both. There is a sheet of water at almost every turn of the road.

The whole scene is incredible to any game-fisher worth his salt. Some lochs are inlets from the sea, some are landlocked and some range from pure fresh water to brackish water nearer the ocean. Thus it is possible to catch brown trout and sea trout and some pink-fleshed trout somewhere between. (It has only recently been established anyway that the brown trout and sea trout are both of the same species except that one decided to migrate to the sea and the other to become a resident in fresh water.) There are also hundreds of sea-pools holding big sea trout.

So labyrinthine is the geography of Loch Scadavay which is only four miles long and two miles broad that the ins and outs of the shoreline give a total of fifty miles. You can see the effect of this water-spattered area if you climb the 625 feet of Beinn Mhor opposite Harris.

There is really only one dilemma for a stranger who wishes to fish the Uists — which water to choose. He could pick a different loch every day and still not cover all of them — not even in North

Uist itself. I have not heard of any loch which has no fish. All have trout or sea trout and some of the more exclusive waters have salmon, not monsters, but lovely fighting fish of 7 to 8lb. There are three rules in my estimation which the angler intending to fish in this paradise should observe:

1 Make a reservation in advance. The local tourist offices at Lochmaddy or Lochboisdale will gladly send information about fishing hostels, angling clubs and sporting estates.

2 Although much of the fishing is free, and in many cases nobody will trouble the angler if he is fishing fairly, the more exclusive waters are owned or managed by the estates or the hotels or one of the angling clubs. I would therefore recommend an early booking at the Lochmaddy or the Lochboisdale hotels. They are fishing hotels with access to their own waters and they specialise in catering for anglers.

3 There is no fishing on Sunday at any time anywhere. The Hebrideans are very strict about this.

Of course, this does not say that the footloose angler without a prior reservation cannot fish. The North Uist Angling Club welcomes visitors and the charges per day or per week are very moderate. Certainly North Uist does not quite have the sea trout fishing that is world-famous in South Uist but where it scores is in the excellence of its salmon fishing on the lochs. Although the usual run of these salmon is in the six or seven pound class, it is only fair to record the fish of 33lb caught by Colonel Craven from a boat on Loch Skealtar in 1932. In 1961 Father John Morrison from South Uist was on a visit to the north part of the island when he caught in the same loch a salmon of 29lb 2oz. Casts of both these fish are on display in the Lochmaddy Hotel.

Loch Skealtar is not far from the hotel at Lochmaddy. It is entirely a salmon water with only a short run to the sea and in a dry spell hundreds of fish are splashing around waiting to get up to spawn.

While North Uist does not have so many of the famous sea trout-bearing machair lochs that are the delight of anglers in South Uist, there are nevertheless magnificent waters like Loch Na Clachan in the west which is entirely a sea trout loch. Other splendid waters are Hoste Loch Eaval. Loch Obisary is another sea trout loch where although the average fish comes out at 2lb the record so far is 12lb.

About a third of North Uist is covered by water. Considering the sheer number of lochs, the haphazard way nature has sprinkled them all over the area, the fact that some have brown trout, some sea trout and some salmon, it would be lengthy, boring and — considering the Gaelic names — bewildering to list all of them or even to try and give directions from afar. It is for these reasons that my advice to a visiting angler is valid — book into a fishing hotel and stay indoors on Sundays.

OTHER ISLANDS IN THE AREA

Berneray is a name given to a few small islands in the Hebrides. The largest and best-known is an island 3 miles by 2 miles in the Sound of Harris just north of North Uist. It is a verdant, lovely place with few inhabitants and is privately-owned, as is its fresh water loch Loch Bruist right in the middle of the island. Berneray is virtually littered with prehistoric remains.

The *other* Berneray is a very different island and lies at the bottom of the Outer Hebrides chain south of Barra. The name means 'Bjorn's island'. It takes the full force of the Atlantic gales and in some of these storms it has been known for small fish to be blown up with the surf to land by the lighthouse 660 feet up the cliffs!

The Monach Isles is a group of five islands which lie six miles west of North Uist. They are very flat, rising only fifty feet above sea level, uninhabited now but they occasionally provide shelter for lobster fishermen who use the deserted ruins.

St Kilda is a small group of rugged islands thirty-four miles north-west of North Uist. They are very remote, very wild and until the inhabitants appealed to the British Government in 1930 to be evacuated, they had lived in isolation for a thousand years.

Today the Ministry of Defence, the Nature Conservancy Council and the National Trust for Scotland all have a hand in the management of the islands and their wildlife.

There is a tale that if St Kildans found one of their group had committed murder, they tied him to a board and floated him out to sea with a fish fastened to his throat so that the gannets killed him.

Other islands in the St Kilda group are Dun, Hirta and Stac Lee. Much further out in the Atlantic is Rockall.

Dear Doctor Zehnder — Come To South Uist

Dear Hugo,

It seems only yesterday since we were fishing the estuary of the Ythan at Newburgh in Aberdeenshire with your two sons. Yet it was five years ago and since then you and your family have been chasing sea trout all over Europe. I think it would be fair to say that you are — all of you — sea trout fanatics, and there is hardly a water you will not fish if there is a chance of catching a few of these Princes of Fish.

Now I want to recommend an area which you have not yet explored — the island of South Uist in the Outer Hebrides. Of course, I had been hearing and reading for years about the glories of fishing the Uist lochs but I had the privilege of discovering them myself only recently.

You know where they are, don't you? North and South Uist with Benbecula in the middle is now virtually all one angler's paradise since they opened that road-causeway right through the 'spine' of these islands. You will find it on a map of the Western Isles off the west coast of Scotland. North Uist does have some wonderful salmon and even more wonderful brown trout fishing, but it is to South Uist I recommend you and your sons go for what has been described as the finest sea trout fishing in the world. And the time to book with the South Uist Estate or the hotel at Lochboisdale is *now*. You can never be too early in making reservation on South Uist.

In very general terms the fishing on the island runs like this. The east side is indented by the sea of the Minch. There are sea-lochs galore and some excellent fishing although much of the freshwaters are peaty from the moorland-rocks-peat terrain. It is on the west side of the island that the best sea trout fishing is to be had. This is where there are the famous machair lochs. These are lochs quite near the Atlantic right down the twenty-two miles of the shore's length which have the same shell-sand surrounds and beds as the vast beaches facing the sea. Down this length are spread a host of lochs abounding in birds, brown trout, salmon and sea trout.

Although it is the sea trout fishing which I recommend to you, get ready for a surprise if a salmon takes your fly. One day in 1964 an angler on Loch Barr caught nine salmon weighing sixty-three pounds.

92

These machair lochs are a delight even just to see let alone fish them. In the springtime and early summer the meadows around them are a blaze of colour when the wild flowers are in bloom. I am told that the Queen likes to visit these waters — so you are in good company.

It would be difficult to advise you from this distance which particular water to fish. When you get there, you will be drowned with advice, particularly at the hotel or on the estate. The most famous stream for its big sea trout is the Howmore system of waters, although drought in the pools may present a poor showing of fish in dry weather. Salmon and sea trout start coming in at the beginning of July and their runs extend through to the end of October when the season ends.

Lochboisdale Hotel offers nine boats on seven lochs (with a maximum of two boats per loch) in three systems, with each angler being allocated daily, according to a roster, a boat on a particular loch. In 1989 on these hotel lochs there were some good catches:

4 sea trout weighing 11.75lb, 1 salmon weighing 7lb.
2 sea trout weighing 5.5lb, 2 salmon weighing 10lb.
5 salmon weighing 30.25lb.
4 sea trout weighing 12lb, 2 salmon weighing 11.5lb.
3 sea trout weighing 9.5lb, 1 salmon weighing 8.5lb.

In 1989 the best sea trout weighed 10.5lb and the best salmon 16.75 lb.

The three-year average up to 1989 is 220 sea trout averaging 2.5lb and 125 salmon averaging 6.18lb. In 1989 over 40 sea trout of 5lb or better were taken.

Don't be put off by the size of the salmon, by the way. Hebridean salmon are always smallish but their fighting qualities are such that a ten-pounder just about equals a Tay or Spey monster in challenge.

You may think that I am going a bit 'over the top' in my enthusiasm for the fishing on South Uist, but I can assure you that it is a sea trout area unsurpassed anywhere else in Europe. They say there are 190 lochs on the island including the small lochans and some of these have not been fished in living memory.

Although I heartily recommend reserving the estate or hotel waters, you may not wish to stay at the hotel. The South Uist Angling Club with its 400 members has rights from the proprietors of certain lochs which they share. They welcome visitors and their charges are very modest. I would certainly recommend that you buy the book *700 lochs — a guide to trout fishing on South Uist* written by Captain John Kennedy, fishery manager on the estate and obtainable from the estate or from Lochboisdale Hotel.

But it is the machair lochs you will enjoy most — especially for the sea trout. These lovely lochs have firm, sandy bottoms and they are quite safe for wading, and since they are so close to the sea on the western side, this accounts for the large and world-famous sea trout. The two main Howmore lochs lie about six miles north of Kildonan. They are lochs Roag and Fada. The Howmore river connects Roag with the sea. Up until now the largest recorded sea trout came from Roag in 1965; it was 14lb and was caught by a schoolboy of fourteen.

Now, how do you get there? Well, I know that you fly all over the place hunting for sea trout, so getting to the Outer Hebrides by air will be no problem. With connections from London or Glasgow or Edinburgh you can fly to the airport at Benbecula. Of course, that leaves you with the problem of hiring a car which is essential in the Hebrides.

Why not take the longer — and much more interesting trip — by sea? Motor to Oban in the Western Highlands, take your car on the ferry across to Lochboisdale and there you are. The sea trip is about five hours and, believe me, a wonderful adventure in itself. There are full catering facilities aboard.

Now — about flies. For the sea trout, I would recommend Blue Charm, Stoat's Tail, Black Pennel, Blue Zulu, Mallard and Claret, size 10 to 8.

Hugo, stop hunting all over Europe for the best sea trout fishing. It is right here in the Western Isles of Scotland.

Where to Get Permission to Fish
NORTH UIST
FRESHWATER FISHING
Of the hundreds of lochs and lochans in North Uist, those best for fishing are controlled by five bodies to whom application should be made for permission to fish. These are:
Lochmaddy Hotel, Lochmaddy, North Uist, Hebrides. (Lochmaddy 331)

The Secretary, North Uist Angling Club, 19 Dunossil Place, Lochmaddy, North Uist.
Department of Agriculture and Fisheries, Area Office, Balivanich, Benbecula. (Benbecula 2346)
D.J. MacDonald, 8 Clachan Sands, Lochmaddy, North Uist. (Lochmaddy 227)
North Uist Estate, The Estate Office, Lochmaddy, North Uist. (08763 329)

SOUTH UIST
FRESHWATER FISHING
Lochboisdale Hotel in conjunction with South Uist Estates Ltd controls many of the excellent salmon, sea trout and brown trout fishings on the lochs. Contact Lochboisdale Hotel, Lochboisdale, South Uist, Western Isles PA8 5TH (08784 332 and 367)
BROWN TROUT
There are twelve boats on as many lochs with each angler being allocated daily, according to a roster, a boat on a particular loch.

SEA TROUT AND SALMON
There are nine boats on seven lochs (with a maximum of two boats per loch), in three systems, with each angler being allocated daily, according to a roster, a boat on a particular loch.
The South Uist Angling Association also has waters and permits and information can be obtained from:
The Secretary, SUAC, The Surgery, Griminish, Benbecula.
Lochboisdale Tourist Office, Lochboisdale.
The Post Office, Greagorry, Benbecula.

Harris
It is when you meet the people in Harris that you form prejudiced, sexist, racist, generalised opinions that do nobody any good. For me, they only confirmed what I had long thought about this place in the Outer Hebrides which some call an island but those who look at the map know is separated from Lewis by the skin of its teeth.

The people are kind enough. Indeed some of them are very generous to a stranger considering the problems of making a living of some kind in such a rock-encrusted environment where there is virtually no industry except tourism and some fishing. Also to be taken into account is the number of times they have been cheated, exploited and abandoned by their leaders.

I have the impression that there are three kinds of people on Harris. First there are the 'white settlers' — the men, that is — who came up from England to escape the rat race or a washed-out career. Many have built or bought guest houses with the help of grants or subsidies. Then there are their wives who hate the place because of the hard work and scarcity of amenities and would return back to the south by the next boat if their husbands would give it all up. You usually find them in the kitchen working their backs off for eighteen hours a day. The third group are the native Gaels who let the English entrepeneurs get on with it and then get back to their own occupations of poaching or river-watching or both.

My wife and I met all three types when we motored down from Stornoway across the Great Divide and virtually into another world. Whereas Lewis is all moorland and lovely beaches and peat-hags and lochs and isolated little villages, the majesty of the mountains of Harris took our breath away. By the time we passed Balallan we knew we were in another kind of country altogether, a sort of Hebridean Tibet. And, of course, it was raining.

The main road south from Lewis — virtually the spine of the whole island — alternates between an ordinary two-way affair and single track with passing places. And there seems to be a car coming in the opposite direction speeding at a priority pace round every bend and over every little hill. And there are plenty of these, believe me!

Tarbert itself is right in the slender neck that joins north and south Harris. Indeed, by looking first one way then the other you are looking at two different seas called east and west Loch Tarbert. It is the place where Caledonian MacBrayne ferries call, there is a hotel, and a few straggly shops but not much more.

As we left this rather desolate little place (it was still raining) I tried to be the Devil's Advocate and see the situation from the local inhabitants' point of view. Who says they have to be — what do we call it? — enterprising? Who needs it? If you're saying, Mr Southerner, that the people in Harris are missing out in sophisticated living and modern amenities, why are *you* here? Why did you come up here if life was all that wonderful in West One?

Off the Cumbraes in the Firth of Clyde.

Young holiday anglers on Bute.

The waters off Arran are ideal for dinghy.

Fishing a Hebridean loch.

One of Islay's 'undiscovered' beaches.

Wading out in an island loch.

Bunessan, Mull.

Castlebay, Barra.

Typical of the many lochs on South Uist.

The author by a loch in South Uist.

. . . and casting a fly on the loch.

Amhuinnsuidhe Castle, famous sporting hotel for anglers on Harris.

Some instruction for young anglers in Amhuinnsuidhe.

A sea trout is 'turned over' on Lady's Loch at Amhuinnsuidhe.

The author with Tom the ghillie in Harris.

Stornoway Castle and harbour.

Starting point for Stornoway sea anglers.

A convenient croy for fishing from the bank on a Lewis loch.

The Cuillin Hills of Skye near Sligachan.

Loch Dunvegan and the MacLeod's Tables, Skye.

Oronsay . . . the wee island off Colonsay.

More water than land on Benbecula.

The Old Man of Hoy, Orkney.

Papay Ferry, Orkney.

One of the many sea trout bays and voes in Shetland.

Brae in Shetland.

'There's a fish rose – right over there!', the ghillie advises his visitor on a Hebridean loch.

So stop criticising our way of life. If you feel we're not all that keen on hard work and like a dram now and then, what's wrong with that? You couldn't have been all that keen on your work or you'd never have come here in the first place. Oh — and another thing — *don't* try to make our Sundays like the ones you left down south. We like our Sabbath the way it is, thank you.

We got to our guest house by a very twisty road round the cliff-edge of magnificent seascapes. The people who ran it were true to type. They were English and very energetic. He had retired early from being 'Something in the City' and his long-suffering wife seemed to be in the kitchen all day long and every day. The meals were wonderful and the accommodation very comfortable. There were seven other guests who spent their days hill-walking, bird-watching and taking photographs.

I wanted to do some trout fishing. No problem, he said. He had the lease of a trout loch somewhere in the hills. A bit of a walk. With rubber waders and a haversack and a rod and a net and a hefty storm coat? No, thanks.

How about a shot at the salmon or sea trout? Ah, that's better. Where? Down in south Harris. Make a telephone call to the pub owner there because he has the lochs. Great. How far is it? Twenty-odd miles round the east coast road.

Sure enough, I did get a good day's fishing. It was a nice loch and I picked up a fishing friend who was caravanning with his wife in the area. My invitation was a godsend. Yes, he would come along. No charge, said the pub owner — just take care of the ghillie. Very decent.

The ghillie was in his thirties, married with two children and came originally from Edinburgh. A nice, compact fellow who had two jobs — ghillie and keeping the poachers off the waters at night for the pub owner. He apologised for being a little late and red-eyed; he had just got out of bed since he had been on watch all night on one of the waters.

Salmon poaching in this part of Harris is quite a business. It had now got so bad on some of the more private and exclusive estates that the factors could no longer employ river watchers who were locals. Most of them had relatives who were at the poaching. The watchers therefore suffered from a kind of schizophrenia. So the estates were now employing ex-SAS men from the mainland.

The Mill Loch was a small loch with a narrow exit to the sea and a roaring inflow of freshwater from a bigger loch further up the hill. The salmon and sea trout came in from the sea, rested or thrashed around the loch then made their spawning run through the torrent upstream to the larger loch.

We had a glorious day's fishing. My friend Douglas caught three salmon and lost them. No carelessness on his part; they simply got off as salmon often do on lochs. I got a few nice sea trout. We were in a hurry to get back to our guest house in time for dinner at seven so we took the west coast road. It was a tortuous, heart-stopping, driver's nightmare, but very beautiful.

Particularly during that twisting, cliff-hanging journey up the east coast, it seemed to me that Harris is a place that doesn't care much about anything or anyone. English incomers, foreign tourists and even strangers like us from the mainland of Scotland are like passers-by in a time-warp of a Hebridean twilight. Nobody paid us much attention and that is as it should be.

The mountains and the lonely, deserted beaches, the wave-torn cliffs and the sun-dappled lochs are the true Harris. All the rest — including us — are tolerated appendages.

Fishing to Suit Everyone's Taste and Pocket on Harris

There are some islands around Scotland where you can take your fishing rod, pick up a permit from someone or other (usually the local hotel) and start fishing. I am thinking of the islands in Orkney, for instance, or those in the Shetland group and many others in the Hebrides.

To a small degree this is the case on Harris. It all depends what level of game fishing you want. Yes, it is possible to fish here and there *ad lib* in Harris and catch plenty of half-pound trout. At almost every turn of the labyrinthine roads through the mountains, there is a loch or a tarn just waiting for a fly to be cast on the water. And as a rule, the local hotels and guest houses will willingly give permission. Of course, although the trout are smaller than those further north in Lewis, from some of these countless waters come the occasional big ones of two or three pounds.

The other kind of game fishing, however, cannot really be tackled on Harris in this casual way. I mean the good salmon and sea trout angling. Most of this is in the hands of the estates and some by hotels. And the only sure way of getting first-class fishing with some exclusiveness is to make a reservation about a year in advance. The fishing on the estate waters is of this character — highly valued, well managed and much in demand by those who do not mind the trouble and expense of getting there, to say nothing of the price of the fishing.

A typical example of this sort of good fishing is in the North Harris Fishery which is in a magnificent wilderness area of 30,000 acres, most of it mountainous. The two most important rivers on the estate are the Voshimid and the Ulladale. The former has been described as the finest salmon and sea trout stream in Britain. That says something for a stream only four miles long although most of the fishing is done on Loch Voshimid.

Like the Voshimid, the Ulladale's main venue is the loch itself which is in two sections — the upper one mainly being salmon and the lower principally sea trout.

Rain, of course, is the governing natural factor on both these rivers. This is particularly true of the Ulladale which rises to the west of Voshimid. In dry weather the run of water, in angling terms, is pathetic. but a few hours rain can bring a rushing torrent down to the loch, urging the fish to spawn quickly.

Nearly all the salmon in the North Harris Fishery are grilse or second-year fish weighing no more than 9lb, most of them in the 5 to 6lb range. The best time to catch the spawning run is from June to mid-July.

Sea trout run in the waters at around the same time, perhaps a little later. They are usually in the 1 to 2lb range although fish up to 5lb have been taken from time to time. What was probably one of the best years for anglers on this fishery was 1977 when ten rods fishing from five boats for four days in late July caught 100 salmon and fifty-three sea trout. Seventy of the salmon were caught on Loch Voshimid.

What is reckoned to be the smallest salmon and sea trout loch in the world is in South Harris. It is called the Laxadale Loch and is in that part of the Laxadale river system which runs north-west in the centre of South Harris and flows through two miles of sand and sea-pools at Luskentyre Bay to the ocean.

The Laxadale River, even at the best of times, is little more than a peat-stained ditch but — and this is important — the salmon and sea trout leap their way through it as if they were in the pools of a large river.

The loch is a deep, weedy water and fishes well when there is a good breeze to ripple the surface. Fincastle Loch, which is an artificial dammed water, is in the same Laxadale system and fishes well for sea trout, the average weight of which are 2lb. There is a hatchery by the Laxadale River which incubates about 100,000 sea trout and salmon eggs each year.

Another fishery worth mentioning is Horsaclett. This is a series of waters in such a natural system that it is difficult to know if it is a river or simply a series of interconnected lochs.

Horsaclett is south of Tarbert running from west to east. There are five main lochs and many other side lochans in an area of boggy moorland. The fishing here is controlled by Horsaclett Lodge and let to tenants by the fortnight or more.

Although it is part-and-parcel of Lewis, Harris is often described as an 'island'. There is such a wide difference in scenery, the types of fishing waters and in the culture of the people, the word 'island' is not so out of place although it is wrong in terms of geography. Certainly South Harris is *almost* an island considering that it is a very narrow neck of land at Tarbert which joins the area with North Harris as if by the skin of its teeth. (Indeed, the word 'Tarbert' means a narrow neck of land dividing water.)

And it is in South Harris that most of the fishing is available easily to tourists and visitors. The Harris Hotel at Tarbert, for example, has some excellent waters, notably those in the Laxadale chain mentioned above. The lower of these lochs get the first of the salmon in the season. The record fish here (at Salmon Point) is one of 16lb caught by a boy of sixteen. In the Middle Loch of the chain a ten-pounder was caught by a boy of ten. Although the hotel will sell permits for their lochs, naturally their own guests must have preference and many of these guests do book months in advance.

Harris is the sort of Hebridean place where miles and distances mean very little. Although it measures only twelve miles from north to south and about the same from coast to coast at its widest part, the conditioning factor is the nature of the roads. Most of them are single track with passing places. Thus a distance of say five miles means nothing when you see it marked on a signpost. I remember driving with my wife from Rodel in the south to our guest house at Likisto which was only a few miles by road going up the east route but much further by the west route. We decided on the east route and the drive took us nearly two hours! The road was tortuous, precipitous and at times quite frightening in the dusk.

The fishing around Rodel is superb for both migratory fish and brown trout residents of the countless lochs. One of the most significant catches on this part of Harris goes back to the thirties when in a run through Loch Strumore east of Rodel, Lord Cardross in one day caught 160 sea trout! Lochs Langavat and Steisevat are two large waters in the area that have salmon and sea trout. Langavat is over a mile long and also has brown trout whose average weight is ¾lb. Surprisingly this loch also has the occasional ferox trout — that is large trout that have gone cannibal and grown to great size, usually caught by trolling a minnow. Some up to fifteen pounds have been caught on Langavat.

There are many opportunities for sea anglers to catch a variety of fish out from Tarbert and particularly among the islands of East Loch Tarbert. Some of the larger boats will take parties out as far as the Shiant Islands where there are big fish waiting to be caught. A few years ago, for example, Donald McPherson of Tarbert caught a giant skate of 147lb and on that trip he and two other anglers had their tackle broken by bigger fish.

On this 'island' of Harris a visiting angler can take his (or her) pick from catching dozens of half-pound brown trout to wild, battling sea trout or fighting salmon or further up the size scale to monster sea fish.

OTHER ISLANDS IN THE AREA

Pabbay is the name given to a number of small islands in the Western Hebrides and it means simply 'Priest's Isle'. The best known Pabbay lies south-west of Harris from Rodel. They say that the Gaelic bardess Mary MacLeod in the 17th century was banished from Dunvegan Castle for composing songs offensive to her clan chief. She was born in Rodel in 1569 and died at the age of 105.

The Shiants is a group of islands which lie east of Tarbert in Harris and the famous author Compton MacKenzie owned them for a period pre-war. He stayed on one of the islands Eilean an

Tighe. There was once a colony of sea eagles on the islands presumably feeding on the rich harvest of fish around them. Anglers who have ventured this far into the Minch from Tarbert have returned with some monster specimens.

Scarp is a little island off the south of Harris and has the distinction of being the place where postage-by-rocket was first tried. On 28 July 1938 a special stamp was produced to celebrate the intended attempt by Herr Zucker to fire a rocket carrying mail across the water. The rocket exploded when it reached its target and it destroyed or damaged most of the mail. The service was discontinued after that first experiment but examples of the special stamps still exist and are very valuable collector's items.

Scalpay is the second island with this name in the Hebrides. It lies off Harris and is a restful and prosperous island of 500 people. It has an excellent harbour and regular ferry service. Farming and fishing are the main occupations. The island was yet another refuge of Bonnie Prince Charlie after his defeat at the battle of Culloden.

Other islands near Harris are Ensay and Shillay.

A Wee Story from Harris

Nearly every angler I have met loves to tell a story about how he ignored the advice of an expert — usually a ghillie — and scored some brilliant success. 'And you should have seen the look on his face when I pulled in that fish. . .' is how the tale usually ends.

I am no exception. Certainly I never make a practice of defying an expert's suggestions — particularly those of a knowledgeable local guide. Frankly I think it is foolish for any visiting angler to turn a deaf ear to someone who has been fishing these waters all his life. But there comes a time. . .

My wife and I were staying at a small guest house in the south-east part of Harris when a good fishing friend Peter visited us with his wife. They were staying at another guest house in the south of the island.

We managed to get fixed up for a day's fishing on a small loch which belonged to the owner of the local hotel. He was very generous and said, 'Yes, you can fish it: no charge providing you take care of the ghillie's fee for the day.'

We readily agreed and the three of us set off in the little dinghy. Jamie the ghillie was a young, pleasant man who knew all the waters in this area like the back of his hand. And he was very helpful. It was a grand day for fishing and a grand loch, small certainly but large enough to have a fine, rip-roaring stream coming into it at one end and an outlet to the sea at the other.

Peter decided to use his dapping rod with a big Loch Ordy bushy fly. Jamie the ghillie seemed to approve. 'Aye, it's a nice fluffy breeze we have today. The dap should do well.' I decided to fish wet-fly using two flies — a Blue Zulu on the dropper and a Connemara Black on the tail. I was glad Peter was on the dap because this is an old and usually successful trick on a Scottish loch — one angler dapping and the other on the wet-fly. They say one raises them and the other catches them!

Not on this occasion, however. Oh, yes, the Loch Ordy certainly attracted the salmon, there was no doubt about that. Three times there was that wild, heart-stopping swirl as a fish came up for the fly and three times it was abortive. The line straightened out, certainly, then went slack. These salmon simply would not stay on the hook. As for me, I had raised no fish at all on the wet-fly.

After an hour, I said, 'We've been round the loch twice, Jamie.'

'Yes, we have that. It's a wee loch.'

'And I've been casting my flies right into the bank at these bays where you say the sea trout are usually lying.'

'Indeed you have. And not a fish to be seen.'

'And you think I have the right flies for sea trout?'

'Of course you have. That Connemara Black's deadly for sea trout here.'

'So if the sea trout are here and I can't attract them with these flies, what d'you think is wrong?'

'Oh, now, it could be a thousand things — the wind, the light, the height of the loch today. And the salmon aren't hanging on either, you'll notice.'

'Damned frustrating,' said Peter.

Considering I was a complete stranger to this loch, I squared my shoulders and took my courage in both hands, as they say. 'There only *one* thing wrong, Jamie. We're fishing in the wrong places — for the sea trout, anyway.'

He stared at me as if I had struck him. 'Oh, now . . .'

'*That's* where I want to be. . . I nodded in the direction of the stream of wild, running water of the river running through the loch.'

'Oh, it'll be far too rough for them there.'

'*That's* where I want to fish. Let's go.'

Jamie sighed sadly but he did row us over to the edge of the streaming water where it tumbled into the loch. I cast my flies upstream into the current and the Connemara Black was taken at once. My rod bent over and the reel screamed. Jamie netted the fish a few minutes later — a lovely 2lb sea trout.

'Well, now, would ye look at that!' Jamie held the fish up.

Peter was dissembling his dapping rod. 'That's the end of the dapping for me on this loch. You've cracked it, boyo!'

It was not the last of the sea trout in that rushing stream. I had an offer almost every cast but I contented myself with three more silver beauties, all over a pound. Peter wasted no time in erecting his fly rod or in rubbing his chin over which flies to use. 'I don't argue with success.' He fastened a Blue Zulu and a Connemara Black on his cast, both exactly the same size as mine.

Jamie had a task keeping the boat steady in the strong current of the river as it gurgled into the loch but he stuck to his oars bravely while we had the angling time of our lives. Peter caught four fish and I could not resist taking one more.

Jamie was very generous. 'Man, I wouldn't have thought it. And I've fished this loch all my life.'

'There's one question I always ask myself when I'm fishing for sea trout on a strange water.'

'What's that?'

'Where would I be if I were a sea trout.'

Elysium of Amhuinnsuidhe

It was my friend from 'Down South' who telephoned me one Thursday and said, 'Where would you like to be with a fishing rod at the end of August?'

'In the Outer Hebrides.'

'Where's the place you once told me anglers should visit once before they pack away their fishing gear for good.'

'You're talking about Elysium. It's called Amhuinnsuidhe. It's simply the North Harris Estates.'

'Are you sitting down?'

'Yes.'

'Hold your breath. I've got you a week there.'

I did hold my breath. 'You're joking.'

'I'm not.'

'It'll cost a fortune.'

'It won't cost you anything.'

I got my breath back. 'Now you are joking — or mad.'

'Listen. A very good friend of mine who loves fishing and fishy people has invited a few of us to join him at the Castle Hotel at Amhuinnsuidhe for a week. And you're included. He doesn't know you but I suggested you as there's a spare rod vacant.'

It took me a week to get over the shock. It was as if as a golfer I had been invited for a week to the Old Course at St Andrews or as a cricketer for a week at Lord's.

Getting to North Harris Estates is relatively easy. You can either fly into Stornoway in Lewis then hire a car to go down to Tarbert and onward by the single track road fourteen miles to the Castle Hotel. Or, as we did, motor up through the western Highlands by Loch Lomond, through Glencoe to Fort William then down the Clunie road to the Kyle of Lochalsh where you cross by short ferry to Kyleakin in Skye. You motor up through Skye to Uig, get the car ferry for the two-hour trip to Tarbert, then carry on by the wee road to Amhuinnsuidhe. For the breathtaking scenery of sea-lochs, mountains and moors, I recommend the latter route.

The castle at Amhuinnsuidhe was built in 1866 and is now a first class, indeed luxurious, hotel catering for fishing and stalking parties. It is run in conjunction with another famous sporting estate at Tulcan on Speyside. The castle has been built in an ideal, almost fairyland, situation close by a stream called the Castle Burn (although the correct name for this water is the River Eaval). It enters the sea after a series of roaring, tumbling falls over rocks and empties into the bay where salmon and sea trout are congregated waiting to ascend.

The building is beautifully proportioned and faces the dappled bay just beyond a green sward and a small parapet. Along the little road and through the archway are the cottages of local families most of whom work on the estate or in the hotel. And further along the sea-girt road is the village post office and store — the only one for many miles.

Under different circumstances, I would not have been surprised if I had had to pay an entrance fee to see through the castle. Indeed, the reason why they left the imposing front doors locked was simply to discourage the occasional tourists who decided to stop their cars and ask to visit the place or if they could order lunch etc. Some tourists thought it was National Trust property. It was in this castle hotel that the famous Scottish author and playwright James Barrie wrote his play *Marie Rose*, a charming story about an island in the middle of a Scottish loch which 'loved to be visited' and how a young girl disappeared into the Land of Fairies when she set foot on it. When we were fishing Loch Voshimid, Kenny our ghillie pointed out the island which he said inspired Barrie to write the play. Needless to say, none of us went on the island — just in case, as Kenny put it, there is something in Barrie's story!

The party which had been so generously put together by our host consisted of the headmaster of what is probably Britain's most prestigious public school, his wife who is a teacher in the school, five of the school's pupils who had just graduated, an army colonel, three businessmen and one of their wives and, of course, my fishing friend who had recommended me to join the group. Our host, unfortunately, at the last moment could not join us for health reasons.

From a fishing viewpoint it was a mixed week. Many things were against us. One ghillie (there were five of them) said that a serious drought in July had starved the streams and lochs of migrating fish and now at the end of August we were suffering by their scarcity in the waters. This seemed the most credible reason for our poor sport. To make matters worse, Loch Voshimid's water level dropped by as much as four inches in two days. Yes, we had rain — a mere dribble by Hebridean standards — but the little streams connecting the lochs were showing their 'bare bones'. Even the Castle Burn with its attractive-looking dark pools showed not the slightest sign of a fish.

Of course, 'you should have been here in late July' was not an unfamiliar piece of advice. (I wish I had a shilling for every occasion I have heard this sort of thing.) It is doubtful if things would have been any better in July if, as our ghillie said, there had been a drought.

Water is everything for the angler on Harris — even in such exclusive and famous areas as North Harris Estates. During a spate the salmon and sea trout rush madly upstream into the lochs and further into the feeder streams to spawn. They seem to know their time is short. Therefore the visiting angler has to be ready to take advantage of every Heaven-sent downpour.

For all our blank hours on the lochs, everyone managed to get a fish. The ex-pupils, much to the delight of their headmaster, all got a small salmon and my friend got two salmon. I had to work hard to get a few sea trout from Voshimid.

It would be quite a distorted picture of the fishing in Harris to paint it in the colours of our experience that week. A few days before we set off I contacted by friend Roddy MacLeod in Stornoway who, as well as being president of the Stornoway Sea Angling Club and a well-known schoolmaster in the local academy, is also a very capable and keen game angler. He replied to me saying that he had had the privilege of fishing Amhuinnsuidhe only once for a day and he caught twenty-six sea trout. He even enclosed with his letter two of the flies he had used which, he assured me, were deadly for the fish. I used these flies plus my own favourites of Connemara Black, Blue Zulu and Muddler to no purpose whatsoever.

I have always said that the real enjoyment in angling is the fishing, not the fish. And this week at Amhuinnsuidhe was living evidence of it. The company was superb, the ghillies very co-operative, the hotel service and food excellent and the surroundings magnificent. The scudding clouds of mist drifting across the mountains gave us thrills like curtains opening across a huge theatre stage, revealing deer caught unawares and the occasional soaring eagle hunting its prey. Reflected in the four miles of Loch Voshimid, the crags of wildest Harris were indelible in the mind.

The week will certainly be part of my fondest memories as one of life's Elysiums for the rest of my fishing days.

Where to get Permission to Fish
FRESHWATER FISHING

The Horsaclett Lodge fishings offers salmon, sea trout and brown trout fishing which is usually let with the lodge on the estate, but day lets may be available occasionally. Contact Neil MacDonald, 7 Diraclett, Harris. (Harris 2464)

The Borve Lodge Estate fishings, situated at the southern end of Harris, sea trout and brown trout fishing in beautiful surroundings. Contact Tony Scherr, Borve Lodge Estate, Borve, Harris. (Scarista 202)

Amhuinnsuidhe Castle is in the North Harris Estate and has salmon, sea trout and brown trout fishing of a very high order. Contact Miss Clare Champkin at the Castle. (0859 86 200)

The Harris Hotel at Tarbert has the fishings on the Laxadale Lochs on the east side of Harris. They hold salmon, sea trout and brown trout. (Harris 2154)

What was once the Rodel Hotel at Leverburgh is now only a pub but still has good fishings on nearby lochs for sea trout and brown trout. Contact the owner.

Harris Angling Club has rights on seven brown trout lochs and issues day or weekly tickets. Contact the honorary secretary through the Tourist Information Centre or at 18 Scott Road, Tarbert.

SEA ANGLING

the Local tourist office in Tarbert will give directions to visitors about boats for hire from Tarbert and from other small communities along the east coast. Also, any of the hotels can make arrangements.

Lewis

There is a happy land for trout anglers where uneducated fish may never have seen any kind of artificial fly in a hundred years, where the day's catch can often be counted in double figures and where permission to fish costs not merely a pittance but usually nothing at all. Alaska? The Canadian North? Eastern Mongolia?

The place I am describing is Lewis in the Outer Hebrides off the west coast of Scotland and virtually on the teeth-edge of Europe. With its southerly neighbour Harris, it is an island, certainly, but in another sense it is another world where the people are bilingual (English and Gaelic) and you can travel for miles by car or on foot it seems to the edge of the world and hardly meet another soul.

For those trout anglers — even the fly-fishers — who may be tired of long-lining with shooting head lines and lurid lures for rainbows on over-populated artificial lakes or paying exorbitant prices for the privilege of dry-flying exclusive waters of clubs whose waiting lists extend for years, or desperately hunting for a patch of quiet water for a few days in glory-land, I would advise them to consider a week on Lewis where they may fish over a thousand large and small lochs and catch trout galore. Here, there is no stocking from stew-ponds, no interference with nature, nothing but wild brown trout with, by the way, the occasional hefty sea trout grabbing the fly. And, of course, the salmon.

Lewis is the north part of a complete island and Harris is attached to it geographically to the south. It is about forty-two miles from north to south and about thirty-four miles from east to west at its widest. The population is around 26,000 of which 5,000 are in the sea-port capital Stornoway and the remainder scattered around the villages and crofting communities mostly around the coasts. An angler can spend days moving from one loch to the other and hardly meet any of the population at all.

The angling writer James Coutts suggested that in Lewis there are so many lochs, there is probably a loch for every rod on the island. He may be correct. There are over 700 lochs of various sizes from five acres to three and a half square miles. And there are more than 400 of lesser size. Most maps cannot even show them all. Indeed the map of Lewis resembles that of Finland in this connection. So far as can be discovered, there are trout in all of the lochs and although some are overstocked by nature with small fish, there are some holding fish up to several pounds. Many of the lochs, however, produce trout of half-a-pound to one pound. Part of the joy for the wandering angler is that he never knows what size of fish will snatch his fly.

Like most brown trout waters on the mainland of Britain, the season opens on 15 March and closes on 6 October. However, the best months for fishing are May and June with a resurgence of activity in September. Another benefit about fishing in these months is that accommodation is more easily obtained because it avoids the main surge of the tourist season in July and August.

How to get to this angler's paradise? Obviously the quickest and easiest way is to fly by air to Stornoway where a visiting angler from, say, the south of England can be fishing in a few hours. Car hire on the island is the best way of getting around although a car is only part of the solution to the travel problem in the more remote areas. Not all the lochs are near a road and may involve a trek across the peat moors. And, of course, it is in precisely these remote waters that there is the promise of the best fishing. Some of them have not been fished in years.

There is another way to reach Lewis. It takes more time, certainly, but to my mind is much more interesting and, of course, lighter on the pocket. This is by car ferry from Ullapool in the north-west of Scotland by the Caledonian MacBrayne ship which leaves twice daily on the three and a half hour crossing to Stornoway. Advantage? You take your own car and avoid the cost of hiring one on Lewis. And the beauty of the scenery, the sound of the soft-spoken Gaelic tongue on board, the excellent catering service make the trip a short-cruise holiday in itself.

Permission is not required to fish most of the lochs on Lewis but there are certain waters belonging to private estates for which permits are required. On some of these, the charges are moderate enough and access relatively easy. On others — needless to say those waters with salmon and sea trout — the charges can be high and reservation well ahead of time is very necessary. Frankly the fishing on these estates is for those who think of the fishing first and the cost second. Initial advice about all the fishing — free, moderate or pricey — can be obtained with courtesy and helpfulness at the Sports Shop in Stornoway, from any of the officials of the Soval Angling Association in Balallan — a few miles south of Stornoway — or from Stornoway Trust Estates Offices in the capital itself. The estates which have their own exclusive fishings are Garynahine, Uig Lodge on the west coast, North Eishken and Soval at Balallan.

Grimersta Estate is something else, frankly. This chain of lochs and river has been judged the finest salmon and sea trout water in Europe by many far-travelled anglers. For many years it has been the private reserve of a fishing syndicate whose membership is limited and access is therefore well nigh impossible for a stranger. Notwithstanding these obstacles to the visiting angler, an enquiry at the estate offices can sometimes be worthwhile for those with a ready chequebook. The Grimersta yields a salmon and sea trout bonanza in its proper season; the fishings are naturally vigorously guarded and well managed.

For those seeking lochs which require no payment, there are some with a fine record of larger fish. Langavat (the Norse name for 'long loch') is one of them and it lies north of Carloway. Another is Loch Breugach which is happily adjacent to the main road. But these are only two of the hundreds available to an angler prepared to drive a bit, walk a lot and fish one loch after the other.

The late Norman MacLeod who did so much for trout fishing in Lewis and who ran the Sports Shop in Stornoway for years wrote a book *Trout Fishing in Lewis* which has been re-published many times and is still available from the Sports Shop, 6 South Beach, Stornoway. He refers to bait fishing and spinning on the Lewis lochs but it is the fly-fishers who enjoy the most rewarding sport — he admits this readily. It has certainly been my experience and I simply cannot imagine the same enjoyment in these lochs using a spoon or a lure or — preserve us! — worms. I suppose, however, such methods are the price to be paid for unconsidered fishing on an island where nearly all the fishing is free.

I last visited Lewis in June of 1990 and fished only a tiny fraction of the thousand-or-so lochs. When I next return where will I go? To the scores of waters within easy reach of Stornoway? Down through Balallan to the borders of Harris and the rock-girthed lochs there?

There is no doubt in my mind where you might find me with my fishing rod and light haversack carrying the minimum of gear and that is in the north-east of the island beyond where the Tolsta road ends so abruptly. In a way this road-end terminal has a sad story in the history of Lewis. It was one of the late Lord Leverhulme's projects for the island, to build a road from Stornoway right up the east coast to link up with the present A857 at the Butt of Lewis. Unfortunately, like his other enterprises in the Outer Hebrides, this one failed and the road today peters out in heather and turf at Tolsta, just beyond the wee church.

For today's angler, this has resulted in a wilderness area of magnificent trout lochs which can only be reached on foot and which are rarely fished. And as I say, that is where you might well see me next year — if you can even find me in that vast area of fishing waters and peat moors.

The flies I will have with me? Naturally, I will have the Zulus — the blue and the black; then Black Pennel and a large Greenwell (say size ten), and Silver Butcher and Soldier Palmer. If I see any chance at all of a sea trout, I will use a Connemara Black. I will be fishing with a floating line with sinking tip and I will be making a slow, slow retrieve from the bank as near as possible to any incoming stream. Then, when a fish takes — as it undoubtedly will after a few minutes — I will raise the rod steadily, keep strain on him and hope that he may be one of the few four or five pounders which come from these waters every now and then.

OTHER ISLANDS IN THE AREA

Rona is in the very far north and very remote. It is forty-four miles north-north-east of the Butt of Lewis and is almost inaccessible. At various times, map makers have misplaced this very isolated island which shows up as a little dot in a vast space.

Sula Sgier seems at first sight, like Rona, not to belong to anywhere, far less Scotland. It lies about six miles north of the Butt of Lewis. It is a nature reserve for the breeding grounds for puffins, gannets and fulmars managed by the Nature Conservancy Council.

It is the traditional right of the men of Lewis to harvest the gannets on the island. They prepare a boned and smoked delicacy which is exported all over the world to expatriates of Lewis.

The Fabulous Grimersta

The river — if it can be described so boldly — is fifteen miles from Stornoway on the island of Lewis. It really begins as a chain of lochs, flows into one of the Roag sea lochs on the west side of the island. Across the Atlantic by a short distance is the island of Great Bernera. The river always had pools put there by nature but the owners over the years have made certain damming and sluicing alterations making them better for holding fish and for angling.

Rising in Loch Langavat (which means 'the long loch') it is just over a mile long and of itself the river would be ideal for salmon and sea trout fishing even although the fish fairly bolt through it in their eagerness to reach the lochs. There are four of these lochs, the waters of which are kept alive and active by the constant flow of freshwater from the river. The headwater is Loch Langavat where all the fish go to reach their spawning redds in the hill burns.

Before considering the great population of brown trout in Langavat or the tremendous sea trout in the whole chain of river and lochs, a quick glance at the salmon angling is enough to make anyone's hair stand on end. On 18 August 1888 there is record of one man, Mr Naylor, with one rod catching on fly fifty-four salmon in one day. Today a dozen salmon in a day is quite common. And the record bag for any one season was in 1925 when the anglers had 2,276 salmon, 591 sea trout and 271 brown trout. August alone in that year had a total of 721 salmon. The best bag for a lady was twenty-four salmon caught in one day.

So much for the King of Fish for which, let's face it, most of the privileged anglers go. The sea trout fish can well be imagined. And the brown trout fishing in the chain of lochs is also excellent; few come out less than a pound in weight. The lochs are shallow and for the most part have a gravelly bottom. This makes for free-rising fish to the fly.

Getting permission to fish this excellent river and its chain of four lochs for the ordinary angler with a moderate purse is just about impossible. The owners have rented the fishing to a syndicate of about twenty anglers who are allowed to invite friends by arrangement. The whole thing is very well organised and there is a comfortable lodge. The fishery has a manager, of course, and there is an assistant and twenty-five other staff including house staff. I would be scared to ask how much each member of the syndicate pays for the season's fishing.

This very private river and its four lochs were a virtual battleground of controversy some years ago climaxing in physical violence between the estate ghillies and local poachers who seemed to see the fishings as part of their traditional privilege. During the season these ghillies are assisted in their duties by students employed by the estate.

The Fishing Estates on Lewis

Judging by the ever-increasing prices for lets and time-share arrangements on salmon rivers in Scotland, there is no doubt that there is a considerable market among anglers who consider the fishing first and the cost last. One way or another it is quite common now for a keen salmon fisher to pay over a thousand pounds for a week on some of the best beats of the Spey or the Tweed or the Tay. And even the time-share system can offer a thirty-year lease consisting of one week annually for as much as £100,000.

Some say 'And why not'? The market is there and the riparian owners are willing to sell or let or lease. The fact that many of the enthusiastic takers are from countries outside Britain does not seem to trouble either the Scottish owners, the ghillies or other less-endowed anglers. This is probably because those who have rented expensive salmon beats in Scotland for over a hundred years have been 'foreigners' anyway — mostly English.

The equation affecting salmon anglers coming to Scotland has always been a simple one — how much it costs, the time available to the angler, the best time to fish that particular water and, if there is a waiting list, what are the chances of getting a beat? Another factor which has always made or marred the week's fishing is the weather. If there is a drought there is insufficient water and no fish worth catching. If there is a heavy long-lasting spate the water is often unfishable. These are the computational odds facing the visiting salmon angler to Scotland. And money itself will give no guarantee of anything, least of all a good catch.

There is one other consideration in this conundrum for an angler who is used to paying highly for his sport — the distance to be travelled. At one time this was a major factor, particularly in the Outer Hebrides. Now that there are regular air services to these islands which can have an angler from, say, London fishing within a few hours, distance and the cost of travel take second place to the thrill of an exclusive water on a first-class sporting estate.

This is where the salmon fishing on Lewis comes into its own. Angling for 'the fish' (the salmon in the Hebrides is known by no other name) with one significant exception is controlled by the private estates on the island. And these are Garynahine Estate, Scalistro Estate, North Eishken Estate, Morsgail Estate, Soval Estate and Grimersta. On these estates are some of the finest trout, sea trout and salmon waters in Europe; this description has been applied, for instance, many times to the Grimersta.

Many fishing guidebooks tend to put visiting anglers off by suggesting that salmon — and for that matter sea trout — fishing in Lewis is well-nigh impossible. They hint at the high prices, the exclusivity, the almost impossible task of getting a reservation. This can give a wrong impression.

There is a saying that golfers use — 'Never up, never in'. It means that if the ball is never up on the green, it will never be put in the hole. The same philosophy applies to these higher-priced salmon fishings in Lewis and Harris. If a keen angler never asks, he will never be considered. Assuming that an angler and his family or his friends really want to spend a week or a month on a first-class sporting estate in Lewis, there is only one way to find out the feasibility of his notion — ask.

The factors of these estates are very reasonable people. If they were not, they would not be managing them. They are also very go-ahead in catering for today's sporting people who want a degree of privacy, the services of a ghillie who knows the waters and the assurance of magnificent environment in one of the few true wilderness areas left in Europe. This is no land for the 'fish at any cost' brigade or the meat-hunters. These estates cater for sportsmen first, last and always.

Garynahine Estate has the River Blackwater where it is possible to fish by fly throughout the season regardless of the height of the water. The river is split up into two beats and the average weight of salmon is 7lb. Connected to the Blackwater are two lochs — Loch McLeod and Loch Tarbert; there is a boat available on each.

Scalistro Estate is fortunate in having Loch Langavat which is ten miles long and is at the head of the famous Grimersta system of river and lochs. There are also two other lochs on the estate connected with the Grimersta — and the loch and river Suirstavat which provide some exciting fishing.

North Eishken Estate has two lochs both of which provide excellent sea trout fishing. Access to them is by Argocat followed by a short walk.

Morsgail Estate has the River Morsgail which runs out of the loch of the same name into the head of Little Loch Roag and there is good fishing to be had on the names pools as well as the loch itself.

On all three of these estates there is also excellent trout fishing and it is not unknown for an angler to have a catch of fifty in a day. Some have been caught up to 7lb.

Garynahine Estate has its own lodge which was built in 1720 as an inn and has now been renovated to a very high standard. On the staff is a cook and a daily woman and the lodge accommodates eight adults and two children.

Scalistro Lodge Hotel is situated overlooking Little Loch Roag with spectacular views of the hills of Harris and Uig.

All the Lewis estates, of course, cater for enthusiasts of other field sports apart from fishing — deer stalking, grouse and snipe shooting.

None of the facilities on the island make any pretence of being cheap. They are situated in some of the most magnificent wild country in Europe and certainly for the angler provide the holiday of a lifetime.

Sea Fishing from Stornoway

When they run a sea-fishing festival from Stornoway in Lewis they measure the catches in tons. In a recent European Championship festival the 200 anglers who participated could hardly believe what was happening as their rods bent over. They caught 13 tons of fish in three days.

Each August the Western Isles Open Sea Angling Championships are held there and some monsters from these waters are regularly recorded. The heaviest skate so far is 192lb and the Scottish blueshark record of 85½lb was caught off Stornoway in 1972.

All types of fish are caught out from Stornoway: conger, cod, skate, rays, ling, pollack, whiting, dabs, bluemouth, flounder, dogfish, wrasse, haddock.

The Outer Hebrides are among the most favourably situated in Europe for sea anglers. The frequent low pressure systems which sweep across the Atlantic savagely batter the coasts of these islands. Lewis, Harris, North and South Uist, Benbecula and Barra get huge storms in the early spring and late autumn and these pounding waves have created alternatively craggy rock faces and long surf beaches of white sand. All these provide sea-fishing conditions and in the summer when the weather is sunny the scenery is truly magnificent.

It is little wonder that the port of Stornoway in Lewis is the largest and busiest sea-fishing centre on the west of Scotland. No more suitable place could be imagined for the most popular and successful sea angling club which was founded nearly thirty years ago and today is stronger than ever with its own excellent club premises at South Beach Quay. It has probably the best amenities of a club in Europe.

For a visitor to Lewis who favours sea angling there is the benefit of temporary membership of the club and the welcome visitors get is quite unique. Some visiting anglers return year after year to renew friendships with the members and to join their outings.

Tackle and techniques in the islands of the Outer Hebrides are traditional — three-hook paternosters with a lead at the bottom, for instance. Tackle is easily obtained from the Sports Shop in the town and bait is always available either from the nearby sand-flats or from local boats.

History and Pre-History on Lewis

So far I have only come across one book which tells the angler what his or her non-fishing spouse might do while he or she is casting on some remote moorland loch. The considerate author of this particular book deals with sea-fishing and, of course, realises that not every spouse or offspring of such an enthusiast welcomes the prospect of spending hours getting frozen stiff on a heaving boat with half a dozen cheery souls while the wind shrieks and the rain pours.

So far as Lewis is concerned, I would like to emulate this author's thoughtfulness and give a little information which might in turn whet a few appetites for the history and traditional background of the island.

Some things every visitor should know about Lewis are that it is the largest island in the Outer Hebrides, it is the seat of the Western Islands Council and the main town Stornoway has the largest population (26,000) in the north-west of Scotland including the mainland.

Almost all of the island (which includes Harris in the south) is steeped in history and pre-history. There are remains and ruins of historic periods all over Lewis. The first 'must' of these to be visited are the Standing Stones of Callanish which are 2000 years old (some say 4000 years) and they are monumental witnesses to an important population and culture which existed then. These stones are reckoned by many experts to have a link with the many other standing stones and circles all over the north of Scotland. Callanish is second only in size to Stonehenge in the south of England and has some connection with it, although nobody knows what that connection is.

The Stones are on the west side of the island not far from a large bay called Loch Roag — about thirty miles south of the Butt of Lewis. It is thought this bay was the focus of some form of religion embracing the whole of the Outer Hebrides. There are many other smaller circles in the area within a radius of ten miles. These are also quite intact and apparently have a connection with the Stones of Callanish.

The bay of Loch Roag itself is well worth a visit. It is studded with islands and very beautiful on a good day. At Gallan Head there were once whales in such large numbers that the species was called the Gallan Whale and for many years thought to be a distinct and separate species.

Near Callanish is a circular double-layered tower built of huge stone slabs. It is called a broch — one of many in northern Scotland and the islands — and it was in these fortresses that the Celtic tribes took shelter in times of danger. Offshore is the island of Great Bernera which was a virtual battle ground during the land wars of the Hebrides and which resulted eventually in the infamous Clearances.

After the Celts came the Norsemen. There is evidence of their invasions and their settlements in the names of places. But that is apparently all they left behind; there are no ruins or artifacts to tell of their presence. The resident settlers on Lewis were the Picts whose language was a form of Gaelic and there are many remains of vitrified forts used by them as defence against the Vikings. The broch at Dun Carloway ('dun' means walled enclosure) stands thirty feet high.

By AD 850 the Hebrides had fallen to the power of the Vikings and the islands were called by the Scots *innisgal* meaning 'island of foreigners'. Then in 1156 a man who was Norse by ancestry but Scottish in his loyalties took power in the islands and under his rule Lewis, Harris and the other Hebrides began a long period of peace. It was soon after this that the Lords of the Isles formed their own type of rule quite separate from mainland Scotland and laid the foundations of a Celtic heritage which prevails today. This was the clan system which endured until the defeat of Prince Charles at Culloden in 1746 after which the heritable system was destroyed by Acts of Parliament.

Lewis largely consists of rolling peat moorland patterned with lochs, so farming is restricted to small areas and crofts. The two main industries, therefore, are non-agricultural — weaving Harris tweed and fishing. In 1970 a museum created by local schoolchildren was made in a disused church at Shawbost. It shows examples of the island's crafts and traditional way of life, particularly that of spinning and weaving. When it opened, a third of all the villagers were operating hand-looms making Harris tweed in their own homes. A knock on almost any door today will probably bring a warm welcome and an invitation inside to see the expertise of weaving.

At this museum there is also a model of the nearby Norse watermill which has been restored and put into working order by the schoolchildren.

A few miles away at Arnol is a well-preserved example of a Lewis 'black house' built by crofters from simple, ready-to-hand materials. The roof was of turf sods covered with thatch and rainwater drained away through the sand filling between the walls which were about six feet thick. Dorothy Wordsworth, in her tour of the Highlands in 1803, commented on the beauty of the beams and rafters of these houses.

Stornoway itself is well worth exploring. The Vikings pushed their way into this almost landlocked natural harbour and formed a settlement a thousand years ago. The present castle was built as recently as 1850 by Sir James Matheson, a native of Sutherland, who made his fortune in the Far East, a fortune said by Disraeli to have been made by dealing in opium. Matheson purchased the whole of Lewis in 1844 and it remained his family's property until 1918 when Lord Leverhulme — of Sunlight Soap fame — took it over and tried to develop the island economically but failed. He left the castle and its parkland to the people of Stornoway and the castle is now the only technical college in the Western Isles.

In and around Stornoway there is hardly any leisure activity not catered for. There are facilities for every form of sport as well as organised trips by boat or by coach to beaches and bays of outstanding beauty.

Where to Get Permission to Fish

FRESHWATER FISHING

Stornoway

For salmon and sea trout fishing on River Creed, Loch Clachan and Loch an Ois contact the Factor, Stornoway Trust Offices, The Square, Cromwell Street, Stornoway, Isle of Lewis (0851 2002) For Loch Valtos and Laxay River contact John MacLeod, Valtos

Cottage, Laxay. (0851 83248) For Soval Angling Association contact Mr J.M. MacLeod, 15 Balallan. Claitair Hotel, South Lochs near Stornoway has trout fishing on lochs. (0851 83345)

Grimersta

The Grimersta river and loch system belongs to Grimersta Estates Ltd who occasionally have vacancies with accommodation available on the estate.

Kintarvie

The Aline Estate on the border of Lewis and Harris has two salmon and sea trout systems including Loch Langavat which forms the headwater of the Grimersta River. Contact the Head Keeper. (0859 2307)

Uig

The Scalistro and North Eishken Estates have salmon, sea trout and brown trout fishing. Contact the estate office. (0851 75325)

Keose

10 miles south of Stornoway. Brown trout fishing on lochs. Contact Loch Keose Angling Association through the Tourist Office in Stornoway or Mr Smith at Keose Glebe, Lochs, Isle of Lewis.

The Sports Shop at 6 North Beach Street, Stornoway also sells permits for numerous lochs in Lewis.

For waters on the west side of Lewis contact the Secretary of Carloway Angling Association, Carloway.

No permit is required on most of the brown trout lochs in Lewis and the booklet *Trout Fishing in Lewis* shows these.

SEA ANGLING

The most knowledgeable source of information about sea angling for visitors to Lewis is Stornoway Sea Angling Club, South Beach Quay, Stornoway PA87 2BT. (0851 2021) Contact the Honorary Secretary.

The Western Isles Open Boat Championships are considered to be one of the most important set of events in the sport in Scotland.

Mr Richard Collin of Baile na Cille Guest House, Timsgarry, Uig (Timsgarry 242) organises sea-fishing trips and has two boats. One is 14-ft open with outboard motor accommodating two anglers. The other is a 20-ft launch with crew. Accommodation for four anglers. Accommodation etc available.

4. Orkney and Shetland

Orkney

*T*he first time I ever saw Orkney the Wehrmacht was just over the water in Norway. It was in 1939 and as an army recruit this was my first posting. And, frankly, I thought I had died and had awoken in Hell.

It is all worth mentioning now if for no other reason than to marvel at the lifestyle, the tranquility and the prosperity of these sixty-eight islands off the north-east of Scotland compared with the Orkney I experienced that first winter of the war. Those days are now fading year by year into the mists of history and fewer and fewer veterans write or talk about Scapa Flow or the sinking of the *Royal Oak* and the *Iron Duke* or the thousands of soldiers, sailors and airmen who disembarked every day at Stomness Harbour from the *Earl of Zetland* and other ships.

I have visited Orkney since then, of course, and as is usually the case with revisitations after a war, hardly any of the old landmarks and scars are there any more. There are some additions like the Churchill Barrier, the causeway linking South Ronaldsay with Orkney mainland. In 1939 as I remember it, that channel was blocked hurriedly by cement-filled sunken ships.

Stomness was leaden-skied and covered in snow the day our little unit of fifteen arrived. The Royal Marines by mistake had taken all our kit on another ship to the Faroes and we had nothing but the clothes we wore and our rifles. I remember eating my first billy-can meal with two pieces of wood.

We put up as best we could in an old disused distillery at the end of Stromness and anything nearer a picture of The Bastille from Dicken's *A Tale of Two Cities* I have never seen. The snow was relentless and feet thick all over the islands. The cold was almost unbearable. The German planes flew over regularly from Stavanger to try to bomb what they could see of the scores of battleships and destroyers in Scapa Flow, which is simply the huge lagoon formed by the surrounding islands of Orkney. And Lord Haw-Haw broadcast regularly from Germany to the troops of Orkney and Shetland Defences his hope that we had taken the precaution of completing page seventeen of our Army Paybook AB 64. Page seventeen is a soldier's Last Will and Testament.

I am told that it was Winston Churchill in London who stood in front of a map and said, one way or another, 'Orkney? Scapa Flow? That's where the entire British Home Fleet is! D'you realise that *that's* Britain's soft upper-belly? And it's virtually undefended. The German air force can fly over from Norway any time they choose and sink the lot.'

'What'll we do, sir?'

'Do? You'll get troops up there. And anti-aircraft guns. And defend the place. Like this — ' he drew the letter 'Q' over the map of Orkney and the famous Q Plan was born.

Those first months of the war in Orkney gave me many memorable experiences in spite of that gruelling, numbing winter and the constant threat from the German planes and the massed troops over the water. Spring came one Sunday morning and it was like a magic wonderland. The snows were melting at long last, the green patches were showing and for the first time we seemed to stop shivering at least from the cold and started shivering again awaiting the German onslaught. I can remember standing at 2 am on a cliff top overlooking St Mary's Holm as a corporal in charge of seven men and being given twenty rounds of rifle ammunition each for all of us. It was all there was. The Sergeant-Major said, 'Don't shoot till you see the shine on their helmets.'

Q Plan or not, the Germans scored many successes. A U-boat sneaked in through a narrow sound at high tide with only a few feet to spare off its bottom, sank the battleship *Royal Oak* with torpedoes, drowning almost all hands, then crept out again minutes before the tide turned. They also dropped an aerial torpedo down the funnel of a destroyer and they crippled the battleship *Iron Duke* so that she never sailed again.

I remember lying in a ditch with a pal Harry Aitken as a plane machine-gunned the fields. And I also remember attending an Orkney wedding of the same pal when he married Anna Flett, a local farmer's daughter. The wedding lasted three days and three nights non-stop and it was celebrated in the barn.

Over the next six years that war took me to many less agreeable places in the world, but those first months in Orkney playing a modest part as a raw soldier in Mr Churchill's 'Q Plan' is something I always look back on with a mixture of pleasure and pride. I made friends with many of the local people and some of them are friends still after fifty years.

Britain's Northern Arcadia

If someone was to ask me what kind of Britain I would like to see over the next decade, they would get no politician's answer. For all the obvious and agonising problems we have in these crowded British Isles, I would never dream of looking to any politician or party to cure them. I am not too sure where I might look for the answer to the rising crime figures, inner city deprivation, industrial unrest, terrorism, increasing road accident statistics, neglected children and vandalism.

The only answer I can think of is — why can't we all be Orcadians? It can surely be no accident of lexicography that the letter 'o' rather than 'a' is used to describe those excellent natives of Orkney Islands. Arcadia was a mountainous district in the Greek Peloponnese which was deemed to be an ideal rustic paradise. There is nothing mountainous about Orkney because there is no land above 900 feet, nor are the islands rustic by any sense. Civilisation was in full flower here long before many other parts of Europe. There are over a thousand known sites of early civilisations on the islands.

To my mind, all the rest is true. Orkney *is* Arcadia, a British county set in the sea, but so far removed from the rest of Britain in living standards, agreeable environment and admirable people that it is really another world. Even though Orkney is as far north as St Petersburg or the southern tip of Greenland, it has a very temperate climate. The average maximum daily temperature is less than one degree lower than London and the daily minimum average is higher than London. Rainfall is less than Torquay. And at midsummer the sun is above the horizon for 18½ hours.

I have known Orkney, its people and many of its places, at the beginning of the last war and at intervals since then. I have travelled in many parts of the world including some of the Elysian Fields of America and Europe and I can honestly say that to me Orkney ranks closer to a heaven on earth than any other place I know. Why Orkney has escaped the pollution by overcrowding and all the other ills which have beset many parts of Britain is a mystery. The birds and fish and animals still have most of it their own way. The long- and short-eared owls, the otters and seals, the whooper swans, the red-throated divers, the razorbills, the hen harriers, the thousands of guillemots, puffins, fulmars and gannets — all are here as unendangered species.

Other parts of Scotland seem to have come and gone so quickly through the pages of history that there is now a frantic endeavour to save and preserve what can be hallowed or listed or made part of the archives. The Scottish Industrial Belt (who uses the term now, anyway?) is undergoing huge changes from the tumult of mining and iron-shaping and shipbuilding to a kind of Silicon Valley complex. With the exception of a few tourist-centred areas in Sutherland, you might imagine that The Clearances never happened. Even the iron foundry areas of the last century in Stirlingshire have almost been submerged in favour of other modern places of work. Local authorities are busy organising museums to remind their citizens of things that used to be. It is more or less the same story among the north-east fishing villages, some crofter areas in the Highlands, even in the cities themselves.

Orkney is very different. Nothing has turned over the pages of its history with unseemly haste. What was once there seems to be still there. Kirkwall, the capital city by the edge of the mirror-smooth sea is 1000 years old and seems hardly to have changed at all. Stromness, Orkney's next town in size, has been described as 'a narrow passage which one might span with arms outstretched . . . crooked as the inside of a whelk shell, suggesting starlit smuggling and romantic meetings'.

Anyone who might doubt the reverence for bygone things need only visit any one of the 100 brochs in Orkney. They are almost all of them of the same design and built about 2,000 years ago. (To be fair about other people's love of ancient things, there are another 400 brochs in the north of Scotland.)

One of the most remarkable prehistoric sites in Europe is Skara Brae. This is a village built 5000 years ago and is almost perfectly preserved. The houses were covered by a sandstorm about 2,500 B.C. then uncovered by another storm in 1850.

All of Orkney is like a vast open-air museum of the past — from the mists of pre-history to the more recent wars in Europe. A good friend of mine, Mrs Agnes Wylie of Stromness, told me that when she was a little girl she went on a Sunday school trip on a boat out to Scapa Flow and how she and the other children were horrified to witness the captive ships of the German navy all sinking at once. They had been scuttled by their crews and the salvaging of some of them goes on today.

Another relic of recent history is also within my own lifetime. During the last war and certainly after I had left Orkney, a group of Italian prisoners of war converted two Nissen huts into a beautiful chapel on South Ronaldsay. It is hard to credit that the magnificent interior was made from scraps of metal found around the P.O.W. site. As a token of admiration for this splendid job, there is a statue of St George standing guard outside the entrance.

Going back to 1116 there was an Earl Magnus in Orkney (the Norsemen owned the islands then) who was gentle and highly respected. On 16th of April that year he was axed to death by Earl Haakon. In 1919 they found his bones in a pillar of the cathedral. In 1137 Rognvald Kolsson began building St Magnus Cathedral and his court became one of the most brilliant cultural centres in Europe at a time when most of the rest of Scotland was still barbaric. Today St Magnus Cathedral is one of the splendours of Orkney. Three hundred years later Orkney was pledged by Norway's King Christian to Scotland.

For my part, as a Scot, I am very glad that King Christian needed the money in return for pledging these islands to Scotland. I would hate to think that I had to 'go abroad' any time I wanted to visit Britain's northern Arcadia.

Valhalla of the Lochs

Every fishing spot has a snag. The fancy coloured brochures advertising the glories of fishing in Canada tell you nothing about the bears or the mosquitoes. In Norway it's the cost. In Germany it can be anything from accessibility to polluted rivers. In France it

125

might take you all week just to find out where you can fish. Even in New Zealand — well, that's hardly round the corner from anywhere, is it?

Here in Scotland there are snags galore, some big, some trivial. There are wonderful lochs in wilderness areas in the Highlands which produce tiny trout hardly worth the catching because of the acidic soil and lack of feeding. Some glorious salmon rivers are now time-shared and beyond the pocket of most anglers; those that are not suffer a lot of pressure. Sea trout fishing is usually confined to a period around six weeks in the year. Spate rivers are just that — some days in flood, other days dried-up stony beds.

In the face of all those risks and handicaps and self-delusions, it is not hard to describe what most anglers want most of the time. The wealthy are scouring the world looking for a watery place in beautiful surroundings where the game fishing is superb, where there are fish galore and excellent fishing hotels, helpful people and good company, dependable pleasant weather, first-class roads, excellent communications and civilisation within a few miles — expense no handicap. The poorer want all of these things at a price to suit their pockets.

It is hardly surprising that most anglers made up their minds a long time ago that such an Elysium would have to wait until they reach the other world — that is, until they found Orkney.

It would be very difficult to find any real snags worth the name for anglers in these seventy islands separated from the Scottish mainland in the north-east by the turbulent waters of the Pentland Firth. (About a third of these islands are inhabited.) The term 'fishing paradise' is a bit overdone, particularly by the tourist propagandists in various parts of the world, but it is my belief that the phrase comes nearer reality in Orkney than anywhere else.

Orkney is a place for trout anglers. The brown trout, the pink-fleshed 'slob' trout and the explosive sea trout that come in on the brackish waters on sea tides to spawn on the edges of those splendid lakes.

Superlatives get worn out by fishers who visit Orkney. It is not so much the number of fish caught (ten in a day is normal) or the size of them (a big one is 3 to 4lb although a fish of 17lb was caught on Loch Harray), or the back-breaking, chair-strapped challenge of catching them. It is the whole thing — the wide

Orkney sky continuing its splendour to the reflections on the lochs, the pastoral beauty on every side, and the long, long evenings of afterglow which bring out the larger trout.

There are five major lochs and about twenty minor ones in Orkney. The largest and the best-known is Loch Harray — 2528 acres. It is very shallow with an average depth in summer of eight feet. A very welcome feature on windy days are the areas of rocky shallows called skerries which not only provide good feeding places for the trout but at the same time provide calmer shelters for the boat angler. One snag is that these shallow areas call for careful manoeuvring because of possible damage to outboard engines or boats. In one popular bay area which is usually busy with anglers in summer, channels are marked with buoys.

Unlike other parts of Britain, Orkney has retained from its early Viking overlords the old Norse law called 'udal law' which permits free access without hindrance to the lochs. What has to be hired and paid for, of course, are the boats most of which belong to the hotels and some local farmers near the lochs. The Merkister Hotel, for example, is situated on the shores of Loch Harray and is well-known as a place catering specially for anglers.

Swannay is another of the major lochs which, although much smaller than Harray (678 acres), is very popular with locals and visitors. This popularity — to say nothing of the larger size of fish — has brought some unsavoury angling practices like the use of set lines, trolling and multiple-rod fishing. However, the Orkney Trout Fishing Association members keep a watchful eye open for such methods and stop them in their tracks. On the positive side, one angler is on record of having caught forty-two brown trout in a day weighing 60lb 10oz.

There are no sea trout in Swannay because the one burn coming from the loch tumbles over a cliff thus preventing the migration of fish into the loch.

Like Harray, there are plenty of skerries in Swannay, therefore plenty of hazards for boat anglers with outboard engines.

Anglers who revel in the unpredictable could have the time of their lives on Loch Stenness. Trout, sea trout and marine fish congregate together in the brackish waters of this peculiar sheet of water. The outfall to the sea is short and shallow and at the spring tides, millions of gallons of salt water pour in at various periods depending on the time of the year, the state of the moon and the tides plus the inflow of freshwater from Loch Harray. All these factors contribute to providing for the fly-fisherman some of the most hair-raising surprises.

It is perhaps fitting that it was in this loch in 1881 that a brown trout of 29½lb was caught by handline. A cast of this fish can be seen in the fishing hut at Harray. And more recently a fish of 10½lb held the record until 1966 when a monster of 17½lb was caught by Mr Douglas Blyth and there is a cast of this one in the Merkister Hotel. Today it is not unusual to catch trout of 5 to 7lb and it is Stenness fish which are prized throughout Orkney as the best for the table. This is probably because of the highly nutritious diet from the marine life which also encourages an excellent rate of growth.

The next two lochs worth serious attention by anglers are sisters — Boardhouse and Hundland — which are linked by a common spawning burn. Like Loch Watten and some others on the Scottish mainland, the tiny white fly called the caenis or the Angler's Curse, come out in millions in July and August making fishing impossible as the trout are only concerned with these tiny insects which are so dense at times that an angler can barely see the nearest shore.

Boardhouse is the larger of these two waters and since it has no skerries, outboarding is not so hazardous for boat anglers. Hundland, on the other hand, does have skerries but since it is very shallow, fishing in the middle of the loch can be most productive in summer.

It would be comforting to an angler to know that migrating fish in Orkney are as prolific and eager for fly life as are the resident brown trout. Unfortunately, this is not so. Yes, Orkney does have some salmon running into the freshwaters and yes, there are good sea trout available for the catching. But nothing is easy in angling for them.

Since Orkney has no spawning rivers or large streams to attract sea trout, these fish tend to congregate in the bays and inlets along the coastline. For the all-year-round angler, this can be a good thing because the best time to fish for sea trout is in the early spring — as early as 25 February, the opening day — and the autumn as late as the end of October when the season ends. In this way he has the best of the summer trouting then outside that season he fishes for sea trout along the coastline. Large lures and sometimes worms are used. The best plan for a visiting angler is to accompany a local sea trout fisher to his favourite spot, if he can get an invitation!

Since I only had one brief — and almost lethal — experience of sea fishing in Orkney, I contacted John Geddes who is secretary of the Orkney Islands Sea Angling Association. This is how he described the sea angling opportunities:

'The fishing in these parts is mainly cod and ling with some pollack and coalfish (although most of these are undersized). We get occasional double figure cod, and the ling can run to 30lb and more (although not many of them). Haddock have been largely cleaned out by the inshore boats but sometimes we hit it lucky. It has been a few years since anyone has caught a halibut, however there is always a possibility.

'We fish mainly on the drift, although we intend to experiment with anchoring over the Scapa Flow wrecks (mainly the First World War German Fleet) in the near future. On the occasions we visit the Pentland Firth, wire line is the preferred method due to the fast tides and deep water and requiring leads of 1.5 to 2lb which can easily be obtained at the local tackle shop. A wide variety of methods is used with baited spoons and pirks predominating and muppets and redgills as popular alternatives.

'Porbeagle shark frequent our shores and many of us have made contact, although since we have rarely used shark gear none have as yet been boated.

'We tend to fish in fairly deep waters, rarely less than fifteen and sometimes as deep as fifty fathoms and almost always over roughish ground. So bring plenty of gear; it should be well worth the effort.

Shore fishing tends to be a little disappointing considering how much coastline we have. However the Churchill Barriers provide a series of productive venues'.

For game anglers there is a small book which I would consider compulsory reading. It is available from the Orkney Tourist Office in Stromness or Kirkwall and is called simply *A Trout Fishing Guide to Orkney* by Stan Headley. Rarely have I seen such an informative, interesting and brightly-written fishing guide anywhere. The author, it strikes me, had fished every fishable water in these islands time and time again. Among his significant catches of 3, 4 and 5lb trout is a turbot of 20lb caught in Stenness while he was fishing for trout. It does not surprise me. For an angler almost anything can happen in Orkney — mostly good.

OTHER ISLANDS IN THE AREA

Egilsay is a small island in Orkney where Earl Magnus was lured by Haakon to 'discuss matters of common interest' then murdered.

Fair Isle is half way between Orkney and Shetland and is a world-famous bird sanctuary. Over 300 species use it as a staging post in their migrations. It is said that the famous Fair Isle patterns of knitted garments were obtained from Spanish seamen whose ship from the Armada was wrecked on the rocks here.

Tide-race

It was Bob Wylie, the local policeman in Stromness and an old friend, who suggested that my wife and I join him in the boat to fish for sillocks and seuths — small fish that are delicious to eat.

In that part of Orkney, Stromness Bay is quiet enough. There is a huge warning buoy near the point and it heaves up and down in a steady swell. It marks the end of the bay before Ness Sound which you can hear round the corner like a roaring lion even on a good day. For anyone out in a small boat, everything is fine provided they time their fishing trip to coincide with the tide coming in. If they are out in that tide-race at the turn when the tide is just going out, the locals say that the first stop is usually Labrador! Anna Flett's brother Eric got caught in a small boat before the war and he was lucky to be carried only as far as Cape Wrath where they picked him up.

I have seen good-sized cargo vessels struggling through Ness Sound against a tide and hardly moving. The wise sailors stay out until the turn of the tide. From the air, when the tide is going out Scapa Flow — that's the huge lagoon formed by the surrounding Orkney islands — is like a whole ocean on the move as it races through the few channels between the islands.

That afternoon with Bob Wylie was one my wife and I will never forget. We had reached the iron buoy at the end of the bay. Bob was on the oars and our boat heaved up and down in rhythm with the buoy. We started fishing. After a few minutes I became suspicious and looked to my right. There was no buoy. I looked over my shoulder and saw the thing already twenty yards away and departing fast.

'Bob,' I said. 'Should that buoy — ?'

He held out an oar for me and his face was white. 'Here — take this oar.'

I changed my seat and did as he ordered. The boat was now really heaving perilously.

'Now row,' he said in a tense, husky voice as he set the pace by his strokes. My wife was staring at us, silent and wide-eyed.

I could hear the water greedily gurgling under the boat as we sped into the thrashing sound and the turbulent waves. I could also hear the roaring of the ocean crashing on the cliffs of the far shore and all the time our boat was being carried along by invisible propulsion. All of us knew what had happened — Bob had mistaken the timing of the turn of the tide. Nobody spoke a word as the seas roared about us; I doubt if we could have heard, anyway.

Wet-faced and breathless, Bob shouted, 'We'll try to get inside the reefs.'

As I rowed frantically in timing with him, I saw to my right the white fountains of spume as the sea crashed on the jagged reefs off the shore. Bob managed to turn the boat without capsizing and we both of us rowed and rowed desperately towards these spumes. It must have been half an hour later when, quite suddenly, we were between the reefs and the shore and the boat was responding to our strokes as we rode the waves like surfers into the pebbled foreshore. Bob and I got out of the boat and drew it up over the pebbles. We were exhausted.

The beach where we had landed was many miles from Stromness and it was virtually in wilderness area. However, we did manage to get to a telephone at a farm and we got back to Stromness before nightfall.

Of course we had a post-mortem. What had happened? The answer was simple — Bob had mistaken the time of high tide and misread the table. The result was that we went out as far as the buoy when the tide was about to go *out* instead of *in*.

There is a lesson here for everyone who sets off to fish from a small boat, whether they are experienced or novices. Reading the correct tide times is vital. A mistake can be fatal.

After all, as in our case, even an experienced local can get it wrong.

Where to Get Permission to Fish

FRESHWATER FISHING

No permit is required for fishing the lochs in Orkney nor are charges made. However, the following message from Orkney Trout Fishing Association is appropriate for visiting anglers:

Although the fishing in Orkney, for the most part is accessible to all, it is a misnomer to call it free. If the trout fishing is excellent, and it undoubtedly is, then this is for the most part due to the sterling efforts of the OTFA.

The Association maintains a hatchery which is supplied by members obtaining spawn from local fish. The hatchery is used as a topping-up mechanism, to help certain waters which have trouble maintaining adequate stocks for such reasons as heavy fishing pressure and/or poor spawning burns.

The Association also keeps a watchful eye open for pollution risks, indiscriminate illegal fishing, destruction of habitats (in living memory three good waters have been lost to anglers) etc.

If you live in the islands, or are just visiting, and you have experienced the variety and excellence of the county's trout fishing, then why not help us to look after it for you. When all is said and done, the annual sub wouldn't buy you one day's fishing on some waters in the South, and hardly buys a round of drinks. So if you are not already a member why not join us now. Membership will allow you access to association sites on all the major lochs and also permit entry into association competitions.

For membership please contact The Secretary c/o W.S. Sinclair, 27 John Street, Stomness.

BOAT HIRE

Loch Harray

Merkister Hotel, Harray, Orkney. (0856 77366)

Neil Spence, The Caravan, Brodgar Stenness,

Loch Swannay

W.F. Sabiston, Loudenhill Farm, Swannay, Orkney. (0856 72255)

Boardhouse Loch
Barony Hotel, Birsay, Orkney. (0856 72327)
G.W. Hay, Castlehill, Twatt, Orkney. (0856 72270)
Mrs L. Taylor, Kilbuster Hill, Birsay, Orkney. (0856 72244)
Loch Hundland
W.L. Hourston, Mucklehouse, Swannay, Orkney. (0856 850449)
Loch Stenness
Standing Stones Hotel, Stenness, Orkney. (0856 850449)

SEA ANGLING
Cod, ling, pollack, coalfish, skate and halibut (British record) are caught in the waters around Orkney. Orkney Islands Sea Angling Association welcomes visitors. Contact the Hon. Sec. J. Geddes, Quarryfield, Orphir, Orkney. (0856 81 311) or W. Sinclair, Fishing Tacklist, 227 John Street, Stomness. (0856 850 469)

Shetlands
Of course I had heard about the glories of sea angling around the Shetland Islands. Who hasn't? Porbeagle shark well over 400lb . . . skate over 200lb . . . halibut around 200lb . . . monster cod and conger and rays and pollack. Recently, indeed, fifty anglers in four days landed 1160lb of skate and 3050lb of other species.

What is not so well known is that Shetland is also a freshwater angler's paradise for brown trout and sea trout.

I went up there recently in the month of June flying directly from Edinburgh by Loganair to Lerwick. I took my two-piece carbon-fibre trout rod, a pair of waders and a wallet of flies, my notebook and my camera.

The Shetlands are the most northerly islands in Britain; indeed they are nearer to Norway than to Britain and much of the culture and some taints of the language are Scandinavian.

It was Maurice Mullay of the Tourist Office in Lerwick who planned my tour of investigation. Right away I was grateful for the hired car. It was obviously essential because unless you plan to take your own car — and that can be an expensive business — car hire is the only way to 'do' the lochs.

I set off from Loganair's small airport outside Lerwick to my first stop, Westings Hotel. It was not particularly a fishing hotel but I cannot imagine any hotel in Shetland not taking particular care of anglers. There are 365 lochs on the islands and every hotel is within easy distance of a voe (a deep cut seawater inlet like a fiord) or a loch.

One of Shetland's star trout-catchers — known for his preference for shooting head lines — is David Pottinger and we spent a day together fishing and talking about fishing alternately. On Loch of Asta we did get the boat out against a very stiff breeze but even with a drogue it was unmanageable. So we fished from the shore and got a couple of fair-sized trout. Then we moved off to Loch of Voe, also fishing from the shore. It was no day for boats. In the face of bad fishing conditions I didn't feel so bad about getting only four trout while David himself had three. The wind simply beat us.

That evening — and there is no darkness at this time of the year in Shetland — I drove towards the north-west and Hillswick on the road to the Northern Isles. I stayed at St Magnus Hotel which is almost on 'the edge of the world' with a breathtaking view; this area is a bird-watcher's heaven. I spent the whole of the next day wandering around the little roads and round the bays fishing the nearest lochs I could see, simply parking my car and unclipping my rod. The wind was still strong and this meant I had to get round to the part of the water where I could get the wind behind me. The alternative was a tiring business — continuously punching out line into strong wind and giving the flies no real chance to be presented properly. I certainly got plenty of trout, all of which I put back; there were no monsters for me that day.

What amazed me was the variety and number of lochs waiting to be fished. At almost every turn of the road there was another shimmering, wind-dappled sheet of tempting water. And it was another Shetland star angler Willie Binns that evening who expanded on this when I asked him, 'Are there fish in *all* of them?'

'I don't know. It would take me years to fish all of them. But I'll tell you this — I've never been on a loch here that had no trout or sea trout.'

'What's your favourite fly for these waters?'

'No doubt about it, the Loch Ordie.'

'That's usually a dapping fly, isn't it?'

'Maybe elsewhere. We fish it wet up here and it's deadly. Early in the season we go for size eight or ten then down to fourteen later. The Ke-he's a good fly, or a heavily dressed March Brown or the old never-say-die favourite, a Greenwell's Glory.'

'They tell me that you're pretty hot.'

He grinned. 'I've had my moments — two and three pounders, mainly. But that's small fry compared with that one over nine pounds from Loch of Huxter in Whalsay recently and the six-and-a-half pounder from Loch of Girlsta. All on fly.'

'Are there any basket limits in Shetland?'

'None at all. All we ask is that the undersized fish are put back in the water.'

'Any coarse fish?'

'None — and we don't want them.'

In the southern part of the mainland, Spiggie Lodge Hotel is run by an Edinburgh couple Captain Arthur Irvine and his wife Rita. The hotel overlooks a majestic, sand-fringed sea bay and Loch Spiggie which is reckoned by many Shetland anglers as the best loch on the mainland. It is big and beautiful with easy wading and golden shores.

When I saw a chap setting up his rod on the west shore, naturally I stopped the car. Who can resist talking to an angler?

'You just starting?' I asked.

'Yes, I am. Listen, I know your voice — you're the angling chap on the radio every Saturday morning. My name's Tony Fry.'

'D'you mind if I tag along?'

'Not at all. You ever fished Spiggie before?'

'Never.'

'You haven't lived, friend. But they won't do so well today — it's too bright and that wind's still far too strong. But when that sun goes down it'll be marvellous.'

'Everybody up here seems mad about the fishing.'

'It's something to be mad about! Over three hundred lochs and some of them hardly ever fished. Virgin waters.'

'Are there any rivers?'

'Not rivers — some large streams and burns.'

'When do the sea trout run?'

'The main runs are in the autumn.'

'What about rainbows?'

'Well, we've tried them, but they don't do very well. Anyway,' he smiled 'who needs rainbows when we have brown trout galore here.'

135

'Is there a stocking programme?'

'There certainly is. The Association stock the more popular lochs regularly with brown trout. Now we're experimenting with brook trout and they're doing very well.'

The Shetland Anglers' Association has published a booklet *A Guide to Shetland Trout Angling*, and can be obtained by writing to the Tourist Office in Lerwick. This guide was compiled most knowledgeably by the members themselves and reading it in conjunction with the local ordnance survey map shows an angler quite clearly the most promising and popular lochs to fish on the mainland and on the adjacent islands. Each loch is well described with access roads indicated and with an accompanying sketch showing where and how to fish it.

The group I talked to that evening in Lerwick were only a small representative of the 500 members but the few hours were hilarious, happy and high-spirited — in every sense!

Cost of a fishing permit in Shetland is merely a token, and it can be obtained in any of the tackle shops. What can be a cost consideration, of course, is simply getting to Shetland. Air travel is the obvious shoice for speed and comfort and the hire of a car at Lerwick or Sumburgh almost essential. Hotel charges and meal prices are quite in line with the rest of U.K.

I flew out of Shetland reluctantly and very impressed. For all its remoteness, distance has never deterred the hundreds of sea anglers who come to these northern islands year after year.

Trout anglers who are looking for fresh, almost unfished wilderness waters seeking 'uneducated' fish will not go unrewarded.

Trout in the Simmer Dim

I got a letter recently from a friend of mine with whom I used to fish years ago. Since then he had got himself married, had two children and now he was asking me about Shetland. Where were the Shetland Isles exactly? . . . Would I recommend them for a two-week holiday? . . . How was the trout fishing and what about this fabulous sea trout fishing in the voes he had heard so much about? . . . More particularly, what could his wife and two children do while he was away fishing? . . . Were there shops? . . . Good hotels? . . . Could he take his car? . . . How would they get there? . . . Fly? . . . Or go by sea?

This is how I answered him:

Dear Andrew,

Don't dream of going to Shetland if you or Peggy and the kids are looking for guaranteed warm, dry weather. Certainly the way the Gulf Stream runs keeps the Shetland Isles fairly temperate but it can change from sunshine to rain very quickly. And don't think of the trip if you want a holiday like one in Italy or Spain or even the south of England. Shetland is Shetland — wild, beautiful, immensely interesting, nearer Norway in distance than Aberdeen, absolutely brimming with sites of ancient history going back 4000 years, surprisingly progressive and modern around Lerwick. And the people are very warm, friendly and they love visitors.

You can fly or go by sea. If you fly you should hire a car when you get there. If you go by sea, you will sail — car and all — from Aberdeen direct to Lerwick which is the capital and main town.

Shetland shares a common latitude with Bergen in Norway, the southern tip of Greenland and South Alaska. But don't be put off with any ideas of low temperatures. The climate is pretty even although there is usually a mild wind in summer.

The first thing you do when get to Lerwick is get to the tourist office. If you haven't booked into a hotel, they'll recommend one, or a guest house if you prefer it. They will also festoon you with brochures and leaflets about where to go and what to see. The reason why I am suggesting that you stay in Lerwick during the holiday is mainly for Peggy's sake and for the children. Let me explain.

There are four main island groups in Shetland — Mainland, Yell, Unst and Fetlar — plus about another 100 of lesser size and most of them uninhabited. There are over 300 lochs. The ins and outs around the coastline just about defy description. There are voes and bays and fiords and inlets, crags, beaches, cliffs and skerries galore. You can gather from this that the opportunities for angling are fantastic: brown trout from the lochs, sea trout from the voes and inlets and sea fishing from the rocks or from a boat. So far as I know there are no salmon and only a few streams which attract some sea trout.

After you have booked into your hotel or guest house, get yourself along to the headquarters of the Shetland Anglers' Association. The tourist office will tell you the secretary's name and address. Last time I looked it was Andrew Miller of

3 Gladstone Terrace. Once with him you will probably have 'struck oil'. They will let you have a visitor's ticket at moderate cost. My next piece of advice about the fishing is to buy that very informative book *A Guide to Shetland Trout Fishing*.

The lochs I suggest you fish are those mainly near Lerwick. Of course you can go much further afield — indeed right up north to the farthest spot you can reach on British soil at Muckle Flugga on the very tip of Unst. There is a loch there if you are interested called Cliff. You are near Bergen here! And similarly you can get right out to the loch on Whalsay on the east or those on Yell or to the north-west at Esha Ness. They tell me that some of these 'wilderness' waters are fabulous. But for you and the family, my advice is stay within a drive-and-return of Lerwick.

One of the largest lochs is Loch of Spiggie which is south of Lerwick; you can reach it and get back comfortably in a day's outing. It is a beautiful loch and is a conservation area for birds. Boats are available for hire by the angling association although the loch can be waded comfortably and profitably from the north shore. It has a sandy and gravel bottom. The surrounds are excellent for a picnic and the family will not be bored. There is also plenty to see and visit in the area. There are brown trout and sea trout up to 2lb in the water.

Another southern loch not far from Spiggie is Loch of Clumlie, again rented by the Association. It is a shallow loch with slippery stones and a rather soft bottom. I would not recommend wading. One of the most remarkable archaeological sites in Britain (the words of the Department of the Environment — not mine) is not far from here — Jarlshof. Although it dates back to 2000 B.C. the name itself, they say, is suspect because it was first used by Sir Walter Scott in his book *The Pirate*. It was discovered by accident when a violent storm tore the south face of a great mound beside a medieval farmhouse of the 14th century. There are eight distinctive phases of human occupation from the Stone Age onwards.

A little further north and still within striking distance of Lerwick is Loch of Vatsetter. Access is easy and there are brown trout of around a pound in weight. It isn't necessary to wade as the fish lie close to the shore.

Loch of Brindister supplies the public water to Lerwick and is quite near the town. Use the peat tracks from the main road, it is easy walking. It is a clearwater loch stocked now and then with rainbows so you can fish with lures and a sinking-tipped line. Again this is a good area for a picnic for the family. Boats are allowed but no engines.

Another water supply for Lerwick is Sandy Loch. The brown trout rise freely although the water is peaty most of the time. There are also rainbows in this water. You are allowed to spin off the west side in deeper water. If you wish to use a boat you have to obtain the permission of the water authority and you will have to row because no engines are allowed.

There is another loch just a few miles south of Lerwick — Loch of Trebister. There is easy access off the main road. There is brown trout and back in 1978 they started stocking it with rainbows. You can fly-fish or spin but you must not wade because it is too dangerous.

Of course, if you *must* fish the voes — the sea inlets — for sea trout, there are dozens of these not too far from Lerwick — Weisdale Voe, Bixter Voe, Olas Voe etc etc. The Association people will tell you all about them.

One great advantage about the fishing in Shetland in summer is this thing they call the 'Simmer Dim'. As it sounds, this is simply the long, long half-light between dusk and dawn. It never really gets dark in Shetland. You can see to fish — or virtually do anything — all night long. Conversely, there are only five hours or so of daylight in winter.

Although the fishing for brown trout in the lochs is best practised using the standard trout flies as you would anywhere, the sea trout fishing calls for other methods as well. One recommended lure is the use of mackerel strip on a three-hook worm tackle. Spinning a small silver sprat or a blue-and-silver or a red-and-silver devon are also favourite methods.

Unless Peggy and the children have good sea-legs and have been out in a boat before, I do not recommend sea-fishing for them. However, you may wish to have a go yourself and there are plenty of contacts in Lerwick who can either take you out in the reaches near the harbour by yourself, or better still, tie you in with a group who have chartered a boat.

However you choose to get out on the briny, get in touch with the secretary of the Shetland Association of Sea Anglers. They are a very knowledgeable and go-ahead body and the secretary will soon have you on a vessel with rod and line.

Some of the monsters they have been catching in the seas around Shetland in the past few years are almost unbelievable. The records show a skate of 226lb and porbeagle shark and conger eels of enormous sizes. The halibut caught off Shetland are famous.

However, unless Peggy does not mind being left on her own with the children most days, I would recommend the trout fishing on the lochs. Most of them are ideal picnic places and many have boats which can be hired. And the few I have named are all within reasonable distance of Lerwick. I have given you only four — there are another 361 lochs all waiting for your rod and line!

Tight lines . . .

Where to Get Permission to Fish
FRESHWATER FISHING

Nearly all the mainland waters are controlled by the Shetland Anglers' Association. Contact the Hon. Sec., Mr Andrew Miller, 30 Gladstone Terrace, Lerwick. The remainder are usually available to visitors for a small fee. There are no daily or weekly tickets as such. Season tickets are available from the Hon. Sec. or from tackle shops or the Tourist Office in Commercial Street, Lerwick.

Almost all the hotels in the islands can give advice and arrange for trout or sea trout fishing. Rarely is a permit required although boats on certain lochs and voes are hired.

5. Eastern and Southern Islands

Eastern Islands

'Go west!' is the best advice you can give an angler who is looking for trout or salmon on the Scottish islands. The reason for this is obvious on the map. West is where the Hebrides are. West is where there are hundreds of islands. And West is where there are wonderful trout and sea trout lochs like those on Lewis and Harris and the Uists.

Of course there are the Orkney and Shetland islands with their magnificent trout lochs but these are hardly *eastern* waters situated as they are right up north beyond the Pentland Firth. For the rest of the islands off the east of Scotland, I doubt if there is one worth the cast of a fly.

This says nothing, of course, for the excellence of the sea fishing around these islands. You may be sure that those thousands of seabirds perched on the rocks and cliffs are not there to admire the scenery. Where there are birds there are waters teeming with fish large and small. And the same may be said of the many seal colonies.

Angling apart, for those interested in the islands off the coasts and in the broad firths of the east of Scotland, here are a few specimens:

Fidra is believed to be the island which Robert Louis Stevenson used as his inspiration in writing *Treasure Island*. The name means 'Feathered island', possibly because of the large numbers of eiderduck which breed on the rocks. It lies off North Berwick.

Inchgarvie is a small rocky islet between North and South Queensferry on the estuary of the Forth. There is no access and it is best seen travelling north by train from the Forth Bridge.

Inchcolm means in Gaelic 'Isle of Columba'. It is on the north side of the Forth, a mile long by half a mile wide and has been called the Iona of the East. A hermit living on the island looked after King Alexander I who took refuge in a storm. In gratitude the king built an Augustinian abbey the ruins of which are still preserved.

Inchmickery is two and a half miles from Cramond near Edinburgh and is now a bird sanctuary for the Roseate Tern. At one time there were valuable oyster beds here.

Inchkeith is off the east coast near Portobello. King James IV who was always making scientific enquiry placed a dumb woman on the island with two babies to see 'what was the original language of the human race'. As the story goes, they were found to speak Hebrew!

Isle of May is the island farthest out in the Firth of Forth and it is the largest. The legend says that St Mungo was abandoned as a child on the beach at Aberlady, rescued by a fish and taken to this island in 516.

In 1658 a toll was exacted from vessels to pay for the first lighthouse which was a beacon burning coal and the quantity used was 400 tons a year. A more modern lighthouse was built in 1814.

In 1956 it was declared a National Nature Reserve and among the huge colonies of seabirds, over 60 varieties of seaweed have been found.

Bass Rock: somehow this stark rock of 350 feet height with its 'blizzard' of 7500 pairs of gannets seems out of place off the east coast of Scotland and so near the shores of the busy, fertile Lothians. It might be more suitably placed by nature in the Western Hebrides.

The legend says that the rock's first inhabitant was St Baldred, an Irish monk of the Columbian church who died in 606.

Since then it has been used as a fortress and a prison by various factions in history. The enemies of Mary Queen of Scots wanted to imprison her on this island but as the Lauders refused to sell it, they kept her in Loch Leven instead. It was also used as a prison first for the Covenanters then for the Jacobites.

The Bass Rock is a seabird's paradise. The ledges are packed with gannets, fulmars, shags, herring gulls, kittiwakes, razorbills and guillemots. Seals can often be seen basking on the rocks.

Cramond Island is the only island on the Forth which is sometimes an island, sometimes not. It can be reached on foot at low tide across the sands. It was an important station in Roman times. In 1004 Constantine IV hid on the island and was murdered by the brother of Malcolm II. At one time there were famous oyster beds around the island but these are no more mainly because of pollution.

Other islands on the east of Scotland are Craigleith, Lamb Islet, Inchcape Rock (Bell Rock) and Mugdrum.

Islands in the South of Scotland

Really the only area of sea in which islands can be placed by nature in the south of Scotland is in the Solway Firth. And there are a few of these worth mentioning.

Heston is an island very close to the Dumfries and Galloway coast on the Solway Firth and it has secret underground caverns used at one time by smugglers.

Rough Island is a bird sanctuary on the Solway coast owned by the National Trust for Scotland and it can be reached on foot in low tide.

Other islands in this area are the Isles of Fleet and Little Ross.

Appendix 1

Historical and Ornithological Notes

*F*ishing husbands whose wives have taken up birdwatching or who like to study the remnants of history will be thoroughly content fishing the Scottish islands. And vice versa, of course (let no-one forget that one in eight anglers in Britain is a woman or that the record salmon of 64½lb was caught by a girl of twenty-two).

The problem with anglers who plan a fishing holiday centres around what the non-angling partner does while the fisher is casting a line. This is no great problem in most of the islands around Scotland, particularly on the larger ones, if the partner likes studying birds or ruins. The opportunities for both these pursuits are many.

History
Throughout recorded history — and long before that — successive waves of different people settled on the islands. There is abundant evidence of communities from the Stone Age, the Bronze Age and the Iron Age, and of the Picts, the Scots, the Celts and Vikings.

Strangely, the one race which has apparently left no recorded evidence of their existence is the Vikings; only the Norse names and a few relics are there to tell us of their presence until they were defeated finally at the Battle of Largs and withdrew forever. For the next three hundred years the Hebrides were ruled by the Lords of the Isles whose headquarters was on Islay; they had their meetings on a tiny islet off Islay called, appropriately, Council

Island. It was a native chief from Morvern on the mainland who gained control of many of the inner islands by marrying the daughter of one of the Norse kings. His son, John MacDonald, adopted the title 'Lord of the Isles' in the 12th century and these Lords of the Isles ruled as kings until the Hebrides were owned by James IV in 1489.

Although there is hardly a Scottish island which does not have interesting relics of its historic or cultural heritage, it is naturally the larger ones and the larger groups like Orkney and Shetland and Lewis which have the most archaeological interest. Here are a few examples:

Arran has a fine scattering of monoliths, stone circles and graves dating back over five thousand years. At Blackwaterfoot there is yet another of those many caves in which in 1306 Robert the Bruce is said to have watched the spider spin its web and which inspired him to try once more to defeat the English in battle. Holy Island in Lamlash Bay is famous mainly because the Viking fleet recouped there before being routed at the Battle of Largs in 1263.

Barra: At Dun Cuier is one of the few Iron Age forts ever to be excavated. In later history, the McNeils were known as the Pirate Clan and the chief's home was Kissimul Castle which has been restored. Parts of it date back to 1060 which makes it Scotland's oldest castle.

Benbecula: some of the island's lochs have traces of ancient duns or forts of the first and second century A.D.

Bute: Rothesay Castle is said to have been founded by the Viking King Magnus Barefoot.

Canna has many relics from the well-preserved Viking ship burial to the remains of an early 7th century church.

Coll: at Arnabost there is an underground earth house of an ancient style that was reached by underground passage forty-four foot long. There are also mystic stones, burial cairns and cists.

Colonsay: here there are standing stones and the remains of Iron Age duns, the most important overlooking Scalasaig which is the island's main village. In 1882 a grave was excavated near Kiloran Bay where a warrior had been buried with his ship and his horse.

Egilsay is in the Orkney group. It was here that Jarl Magnus was murdered and a cenotaph marks the site. Jarl (Earl) Magnus was the grandson of Thorfinn the Mighty, a Norse king whose dominion included the Hebrides, a large area of Scotland and a realm in Ireland.

Eigg: St Donan landed here in the 7th century and there is evidence of him and his monks at the hamlet called Kildonan.

Eileach an Naoimh otherwise 'The Isle of the Saints'. There are what may be among the earliest of all Christian settlements in the entire Western Isles. On this island, too, is the grave of St Ethne, mother of St Columba.

Harris: Although the whole of Harris has many traces of ancient occupation, the most outstanding example of ecclesiastical architecture in the Hebrides is St Clement's Church at Rodel dating from before 1549 when the church was built as a cruciform.

Hestan is in the Solway Firth. Archaeologists have found a large and interesting 'midden' of oyster shells which probably dates from the Mesolithic period.

Inchcolm is known as the 'Iona of the east'. King Alexander built an Augustinian abbey, the ruins of which are well preserved today.

Inchmickery has a neolithic standing stone, the origins and purpose of which are unknown.

Iona has been named as 'the cradle of Christianity' in Scotland, the place chosen by St Columba in AD 563 to establish a religious centre from which he and his missionaries carried the gospel to various parts of Scotland and beyond.

The monastery was rebuilt by Queen Margaret in 1203, then again in 1500 by the Lord of the Isles when it attained cathedral status. In 1899 the ruins were gifted to the Church of Scotland and have been restored since 1910.

Islay: Port Ellen and Port Charlotte are planned villages of the 18th century and in the latter is a Museum of Islay Life.

Jura it is thought, has had human habitation for about 5000 years. There are standing stones, some of which like the Camus Stack, are twelve feet high and were probably erected before the pyramids of Egypt.

Lewis: Loch Roag is in the west of the island and it is thought that this whole area must have been the focal point of religious belief for all of the Outer Hebrides. The colonnated stone circle of Callanish, dating between 1500 and 2000 years B.C. is reckoned to be second only in importance to Stonehenge in England.

There are other circles within a ten mile radius which somehow seem to be connected with the Callanish one. There is also a well preserved Iron Age broch at Carloway standing thirty feet on one side.

Lismore was once the site of a major Christian settlement and St Moulag, a rival of St Columba, based himself here.

Muck: at the entrance to the harbour at Port Mor stands Castal Dun Ban, a fortified rock of the Bronze Age.

Mull is the centre of the long history of the Western Isles. There are many prehistoric sites including the standing stones at Dervaig, a galleried fort dating from the first century B.C. near Burg in the north-west. There are also numerous brochs and Celtic crosses.

North Uist: there is evidence of occupation going back 4000 years consisting of standing stones, stone circles and chambered cairns.

Orkney: These sixty-eight islands are world-famous in having such an abundance of prehistoric sites — standing stones, circles, brochs, chambers. Some are the finest of their kind in the world in terms of preservation like Skara Brae — ten houses covered by a sandstorm in 2500 B.C. and uncovered by another storm in 1850. People lived in these houses 4,500 years ago.

South Uist: like the other Hebridean islands South Uist has its ample share of relics and ruins from history. In particular there are wheel-houses of the second century at Kilphedar and Drimore.

Shetland: Sumburgh Airport is less than five miles from what the Department of the Environment describes as one of the most remarkable archaeological sites in Britain — Jarlshof. Within its three acres is the evidence of people who occupied this place from the Bronze Age, the Iron Age right through to the Viking period — a total of 4000 years. The broch and courtyard and wheelhouses are the best examples of their kind to be found anywhere.

There are brochs and ruins of other edifices and mystic circles scattered throughout the Shetland isles.

Skye: the oldest inhabited castle in Britain is Dunvegan, the home of the chiefs of the Clan MacLeod. The earliest part was built in the 9th century. The castle is open to the public from Easter to October.

Ornithology

Ailsa Craig: a favoured goal for seabird-watchers. Gannets and puffins predominate.

Arran: eagles, falcons, herons, waders and gannets.

Barra: This island has the black- and red-throated diver, barnacle geese, Hebridean wrens and auks.

Bass Rock: The National Trust for Scotland owns this island which is one of the largest and oldest colonies of gannets in Britain.

Berneray: There is a large puffinry here.

Boreray: strictly for those adventurous enough to sail as far as St Kilda on an organised trip. 20,000 nesting pairs of gannets is the estimated figure of these birds on this island. This represents about a seventh of the world's adult gannets.

Canna: 157 species of birds have been recorded on this island including heron, graylag goose, red-breasted merganser, collared dove, sparrowhawk, wood pigeon, mistle thrust, blue tit, Siskin, linnet. Only one species has ceased to breed — the golden eagle.

Colonsay: kittiwakes, guillemots and razorbills breed here. Barnacle geese winter in *Oronsay*.

Fair Isle: Since 1954 the island has been administered by the National Trust for Scotland and is one of the most important areas for ornithology in the world. 300 species of migrating birds use it as a staging post. There is a bird observatory catering for birdwatchers.

Inchmickery is a bird sanctuary and a noted breeding ground for the Roseate Tern.

Isle of May in the outer reaches of the Forth, is an important bird sanctuary and observatory because it is on the main migration route south.

Lamb Islet: a bird sanctuary close to North Berwick, is really a bird rock. The R.S.P.B. have an annual outing to count the birds.

Lewis: although the interior of the island is not very rich in bird life, around the coasts there is an abundance. The skua and the red-necked phalarope breed here at the most southerly of their normal range. Also here are the golden eagle, corncrake, the red-throated diver, buzzard, merlin, peregrine falcon, the blue tit, the collared dove, purple sandpiper, turnstone heron, redshank, wigeon, tern and gulls. Also on these wild coasts are cormorants, shags, gannets and fulmars.

Jura: there are over a hundred species of birds here and practically every known variety of seabird on the shores.

Mull: a local guide *The Isle of Mull* by Norah Turner and Audrey Finlay lists sixty resident species of birds, forty-seven summer visitors and twenty-four winter visitors.

North Uist: the R.S.P.B. established 1500 acres of reserve at Balranald which is a nutrient-rich marsh. Amongst the birds which breed here are little grebe, mallard, teal, gadwall, wigeon, shoveller, tipped duck, pochard, eider and altogether there is a total of forty-three species.

Orkney: according to the R.S.P.B. there are 35,000 guillemots on a brief stretch of cliff at their Marwick Head reserve. This is typical of the teeming bird life of scores of different species all over the islands. Orkney is a birdwatcher's paradise.

Rhum is a National Nature Reserve and is famous for its wild flowers, red deer and birds. The Nature Conservancy Council in 1984 listed 194 species of birds on the island.

Shetland: these islands, the farthest north of any in Britain, are frankly a paradise for birdwatchers who come here from all over the world. The seascapes are wilder and more rugged than those in Orkney but they provide nesting for thousands of seabirds of all kinds, some of them from Arctic regions.

Skye is probably the one island where a birdwatcher will stand the best chance of seeing a golden eagle as many of them nest on the inaccessible cliff faces. Hen harriers are returning to Skye and fulmars nest at Idrigill.

South Uist: Loch Druidibeg is a National Nature Reserve of 4,145 acres. Half of this is owned by the Nature Conservancy Council and is a breeding area for scores of species of birds, particularly the greylag goose.

Appendix 2

Travel Details

*T*here are two main ways of getting to the islands around Scotland — by sea and by air. Travelling by sea, the main ferry operator for the western isles is:
Caledonian MacBrayne Ltd.,
The Ferry Terminal
Gourock PA19 1QP (0475 33755)

The ferry operator for Orkney and Shetland is:
P. and O. Ferries
P.O. Box 5
P. & O. Ferries Terminal
Jamieson's Quay
Aberdeen AB9 8DL (0224 572 615)

TRAVELLING BY SEA
Here are some details of sailings by Caledonian MacBrayne:

Island	Crossing	Sailing Time
Arran	Ardrossan–Brodick	1 hour
	Claonaig–Lochranza (Summer only)	30 mins
Bute	Wemyss Bay–Rothesay	30 mins
	Colintraive–Rhubodach	5 mins
Barra	Oban–Castlebay	5½ hours
	Armadale–Castlebay	5 hours
Benbecula	Uig–Lochmaddy	2 hours
Colonsay	Oban–Colonsay	2½ hours

Canna	Malaig–Canna	4½ hours
Coll	Oban–Coll	4 hours
Eigg	Mallaig–Eigg	1 hour
Gigha	Tayinloan–Gigha	20 mins
Harris	Uig–Tarbert	2 hours
Islay	Kennacraig–Port Ellen (Summer only)	2½ hours
	Port Askaig	2¾ hours
Jura	Ferry to Islay then short ferry to Jura	5 mins
Lewis	Ullapool–Stornaway	3½ hours
Cumbrae	Largs–Millport	10 mins
Mull	Oban–Craignure	45 mins
North Uist	Uig–Lochmaddy	2 hours
Raasay	Sconser–Raasay	15 mins
Rhum	Mallaig–Rhum	3 hours
Skye	Mallaig–Armadale	30 mins
	Kyle of Lochalsh–Kyleakin	5 mins
Tiree	Oban–Scarinish	4 hours

P. and O. Sailings are from Aberdeen or Scrabster to Orkney and Shetland

TRAVELLING BY AIR

Two airlines serve the Scottish islands flying from Glasgow and Edinburgh:
British Airways plc, 66 Gordon Street, Glasgow G1 (041 332 9666)
Loganair Ltd, St Andrews Drive, Glasgow Airport, Paisley PA3 (041 889 13)

SPECIAL PACKAGES

Loganair Ltd offer 'Discover Scotland' all-in holiday packages in conjunction with first-class hotels in Orkney, Shetland, the Outer Hebrides, Barra, Tiree, Fair Isle and Islay. Among other activities, these trips include fishing on certain islands.

Although not specified for fishing, Caledonian MacBrayne offer Scottish Island Holidays of various periods and routes among the 23 islands the company serves. 'Island Hopping' tickets are also available.

MAPS

For those who prefer a complete atlas in book form I cannot recommend anything better than the Ordnance Survey Road Atlas of Great Britain published by Ordnance Survey and Temple Press, an imprint of Hamlyn Publishing Group Ltd 1987. It is approximately 4 miles to the inch.

The individual Ordnance Survey one-inch maps which can be purchased in most bookshops and large newsagents are:-

Islands	Sheet Number		
Lewis and Harris	12	17	18
North Uist	17		
South Uist	23	32	
Skye	24	25	34
Coll Tiree	44		
Mull	45	51	
Jura	51		
Islay	57		
Orkney	5	6	7
Shetland	1	2	3	4

Bibliography

The Observer Island Britain edited by Peter Crookston. *The Observer* Magazine. MacDonald (Publishers) Ltd 1981.

The Salmon Rivers of Scotland by Derek Mills and Neill Graesser. Cassell Ltd, revised edition 1992.

Scotland for Game, Sea and Coarse Fishing Pastime Publications 1989.

Where to Fish 1988-89 edited by D.A. Orton. Thomas Harmsworth Publishing Co.

The Scottish Lochs by Tom Weir. Constable 1972.

Harris and Lewis (Outer Hebrides) by Francis Thompson. David and Charles 1973.

The Fishing Waters of Scotland by W.B. Currie and Moray McLaren.

The Trout Lochs of Scotland by Bruce Sandison. George Allen and Unwin, revised edition 1993.

The Sea Angler's Guide to Britain and Ireland by John Darling. Lutterworth Press 1982.

Enjoying Scotland by Campbell Steven. Robert Hale 1971.

The Companion Guide to the West Highlands of Scotland by W.H. Murray. Collins 1968.

Game Fishing in Scotland by Bruce Sandison. Mainstream Publishing 1988.

An Island Here and There by Alasdair Alpin MacGregor. Kingsmead Press 1972.

A Journey to the Western Islands; Johnson's journeys retraced by Finlay J. MacDonald. MacDonald and Co 1983.

The Highlands and Islands by Francis Thompson. Robert Hale 1974.

The Island of Mull by John MacCormick. Alex. MacLaren & Sons 1923.

Portrait of Argyll and the Southern Hebrides by David Graham-Campbell. Robert Hale 1978.

The Scottish Highlands by John A. Lister. Bartholomew 1978.

Hamish Brown's Scotland by Hamish Brown. Aberdeen University Press 1988.

The Fragile Islands by Bertina Selby. Richard Drew Publishing 1989.

The New Shell Guides 'Northern Scotland and the Islands' Francis Thompson. Michael Joseph 1987.

St Kilda by Francis Thompson. David and Charles 1970.

The Hebrides by W.H. Murray. Wm. Heinemann 1966.

The Island Hills by Campbell Steven. Hurst and Blackett 1955.

Britain's Offshore Islands by Michael Shea. Country Life Books 1981.

A Tangle of Islands by L.R. Higgins. Robert Hale 1971.

A Guide to Eigg and Muck by L. McEwen. National Library of Scotland.

Island Years by Frank Fraser Darling. Pan Books, London 1973.

Canna — the story of a Hebridean island by J.L. Campbell. Oxford University Press 1984.

The Highlands and Islands of Scotland by A.C. O'Dell, M.Sc. and K. Walton, M.A., Ph.D. Thomas Nelson and Sons Ltd.

Hebridean Islands (Colonsay, Gigha, Jura) by John Mercer. Blackie 1974.

The Lochs of Scotland and How to Fish them by Tom Stewart. Ernest Benn Ltd 1964.

Portrait of the Clyde by Jack House. Robert Hale 1975.

A Guide to Scotland's Countryside by Roger Smith. MacDonald Publishers 1985.

Companion Guide to the West Highlands of Scotland by W.H. Murray. Wm. Collins.

The Island of Rhum by Hamish M. Brown. Cicerone Press.

The Road Through the Isles by John Sharkey. Wildwood House 1986.

The Supernatural Highlands by Francis Thompson. Robert Hale 1976.

Foula — Island West of the Sun by Sheila Gear. Robert Hale 1983.

Game Fishing in the Outer Hebrides by James Coutts. Highland Development Board.

Scottish Island Hopping by Jemima Tindall. MacDonald Futura Publishers 1981.

The Uists and Barra by Francis Thompson. David and Charles 1974.

Colonsay and Oronsay by J. de V. Loder 1935.

Index